Paideia Latina
- LEVEL A -

by Rose Spears

ISBN: 978-0-9962648-5-3
Copyright © 2018 Rosanne Spears
Cover art and interior art from *Hope's Greek and Roman Designs* (Dover, 2005)
Published by Madison Street Publishing (Oregon City, OR, USA)

All rights reserved. No part of this publication may be reproduced, distributed, or transmitted in any form or by any means, including photocopying, recording, or other electronic or mechanical methods, without the prior written permission of the publisher, except in the case of brief quotations embodied in critical reviews and certain other noncommercial uses permitted by copyright law.

TABLE OF CONTENTS

WEEK 1: Introduction 5
WEEK 2: Present Tense Verb Endings 7
WEEK 3: Present Tense Verb Translation 13
WEEK 4: Noun Cases; First Declension Noun Endings 19
WEEK 5: Noun Genders; Nominative Case: Subject 25
WEEK 6: REVIEW 32
WEEK 7: Second Declension Masculine Noun Endings 38
WEEK 8: Irregular Verb "Sum"; Second Declension Masculine Continued 45
WEEK 9: Nominative Case: Predicate Nominative 52
WEEK 10: Second Declension Neuter Noun Endings 58
WEEK 11: REVIEW 65
WEEK 12: First and Second Declension Adjectives 71
WEEK 13: First and Second Declension Adjectives; Predicate Adjectives 77
WEEK 14: Noun Jobs 84
WEEK 15: Noun Jobs Continued; PAINS 91
WEEK 16: REVIEW 98
WEEK 17: Accusative Case: Direct Object 105
WEEK 18: Accusative Case Continued; Second Conjugation Verbs 113
WEEK 19: Imperfect Tense 120
WEEK 20: Imperfect Tense Continued 127
WEEK 21: REVIEW 132
WEEK 22: Future Tense 138
WEEK 23: Present, Imperfect, and Future Tenses 138
WEEK 24: Imperfect of Irregular Verb "Sum" 151
WEEK 25: Future of Irregular Verb "Sum" 157
WEEK 26: REVIEW 163
WEEK 27: Ablative Case: Prepositions 170
WEEK 28: Ablative Case: Prepositions Continued 176
WEEK 29: Accusative Case: Prepositions 181
WEEK 30: Accusative Case: Prepositions Continued 187
WEEK 31: REVIEW 193
WEEKS 32 & 33: CUMULATIVE REVIEW 198
REFERENCE PAGES: CHANTS AND GLOSSARY 207

WEEK 1: Introduction

Welcome to an exciting year of Latin! There are many reasons that people learn this language:

- Latin vocabulary helps you understand the meanings of English words since many English words come from Latin.
- Latin grammar will give you a better understanding of English grammar.
- Learning Latin will help you learn other foreign languages.
- Latin is an orderly language and will help you discipline your mind.
- Latin is a historical language, the language of the world that Jesus was born into and the language of the church for hundreds of years.
- Latin is fun!

Two Kinds of Pronunciation

Since we don't have a time machine or voice recorders from the ancient world, no one knows exactly how the ancient Romans pronounced their language. There are two different ways of pronouncing it today. One way is called **ecclesiastical pronunciation**, which just means "church" Latin. This is the way that Latin pronunciation has developed through people using it over time. It is the way that Latin is pronounced when it is said in prayers or sung in music.

The other way is called **classical pronunciation**, which was developed by scholars in the 1800s. This was an educated guess of how the ancient Romans pronounced the words. This pronunciation is used today in scientific terms like the names for animal and plant species.

In this book, we will use the ecclesiastical pronunciation since it is more beautiful to the ear and since it follows the tradition of Latin through church history.

How to Pronounce Words

Don't be afraid to say Latin words! Just sound out each letter and give it your best try. There are no "silent E" or "silent G" rules in Latin, so give each letter a sound. Most of the consonants sound the same as in English, but here are a few that are different:

> C says a hard "c" (as in **c**at) in front of: a, o, u
> C says a soft "ch" (as in **c**ello) in front of: e, i, ae, oe
>
> G says a hard "g" (as in **g**ate) in front of: a, o, u
> G says a soft "j" (as in **g**em) in front of: e, i, ae, oe
>
> T normally says "t" (as in **t**own), but says "ts" (as in **ts**ar) in front of: i
>
> Y doesn't exist in Latin, but when a word starts with "i", then the "i" says "y" (as in **y**et)

The vowels in Latin are usually pronounced this way:

    A says "ah" (as in f**a**ther)

    E says "ey" (as in pr**ey**) or short "e" as in (p**e**t)

    I says "ee" (as in mach**i**ne)

    O says "oh" (as in g**o**)

    U says "oo" (as in t**u**ne)

Dipthongs are two vowels put together that make one sound. The most common Latin dipthongs are pronounced this way:

    AE says "ay" (as in s**ay**)

    OE says "ay" (as in s**ay**)

    AU says "ow" (as in n**ow**)

In each lesson, this book will give you pronunciation guides with each vocabulary word for how to say it. Soon, you will get the hang of it and be ready to pronounce words on your own!

How to Accent Words

All words have an **accent**. This is the syllable of the word that we emphasize by holding it out longer or saying it a little louder. We can show where the accent is by putting an accent mark (') over the word. Here are some words in English and the way we pronounce them

    Forest – Pronunciation: fór-est

    Afraid – Pronunciation: a-fráid

    Wonderful – Pronunciation: wón-der-ful

In Latin, with words that are more than one syllable long, accents always come on the second to last syllable (like fór-est) or the third to last syllable (like wón-der-ful). In this book, there will be an accent mark on your vocabulary words showing where the accent should fall.

Derivatives

English has many words that come from Latin. We call the Latin word the **root** and the English word that comes from it the **derivative**. As you learn new Latin words, try to think of derivatives that come from them.

WEEK 2: Present Tense Verb Endings

Goals: Find the present stem of a verb, recite the present tense endings, and match up present tense endings with English pronouns.

Vocabulary

ámo, amáre, amávi, amátum AH-moh, ah-MAH-ray, ah-MAH-vee, ah-MAH-toom	I love, to love, I loved, loved
cánto, cantáre, cantávi, cantátum CON-toh, con-TAH-ray, con-TAH-vee, con-TAH-toom	I sing, to sing, I sang, sung
labóro, laboráre, laborávi, laborátum lah-BOR-oh, lah-bor-AH-ray, lah-bor-AH-vee, lah-bor-AH-toom	I work, to work, I worked, worked
nárro, narráre, narrávi, narrátum NAH-roh, nah-RAH-ray, nah-RAH-vee, nah-RAH-toom	I tell, to tell, I told, told
óro, oráre, orávi, orátum OH-roh, oh-RAH-ray, oh-RAH-vee, oh-RAH-toom	I pray, to pray, I prayed, prayed

Chant: Present Tense Verb Endings

	Singular	Plural
1st Person	-o	-mus
2nd Person	-s	-tis
3rd Person	-t	-nt

Chant: English Personal Pronouns

	Singular	Plural
1st Person	I	we
2nd Person	you	you all
3rd Person	he/she/it	they

Grammar Lesson

In this lesson, we are learning the basics of Latin verbs. A **verb** is an action or a state of being. Each Latin verb has **four principal parts**. You will need to memorize all four parts. The four parts are called: the present, the infinitive, the perfect, and the passive participle (or supine).

This week we are learning how to find the **present stem** of the verb. To do this, we go to the second principal part (the infinitive) and chop off the "-re" ending.

> Example: Infinitive = amare → ama~~re~~ → Stem = ama

Once we have the stem, we can add endings to it to change who is doing the verb. We have 1st person, 2nd person, and 3rd person endings. In English, **1st person** is "I" or "we." **2nd person** is "you" or "you all." **3rd person** is "he, she, it" or "they." If only one person is involved (I, you, he, she, it), we call the verb **singular**. If more than one person is involved (we, you all, they), we call the verb **plural**.

The first chant you will memorize this week is the **Present Tense Verb Endings**: -o, -s, -t, -mus, -tis, -nt. Next week we will learn how to add these to the verb stem and begin translating Latin words. The second chant is the **English Personal Pronouns**: I, you, he/she/it, we, you all, they. These are what the verb endings mean in English. A Latin verb that ends in "-o" means "I _____." A Latin verb that ends in "-s" means "you _____."

Grammar Sound Off

A verb is an action…	…or a state of being.
Each verb has…	…four principal parts:
Present, Infinitive, Perfect…	…Passive Participle or Supine.
We get the present stem…	…from the Infinitive.
To get the present stem…	…chop off the R E.
What is the person?	The one doing the verb!
What is the number?	Singular or Plural!
First Person Singular…	…-o,-o-o…I, I, I
Second Person Singular…	…-s,-s,-s…you, you, you
Third Person Singular…	…-t,-t,-t…he, she, it
First Person Plural…	…-mus,-mus,-mus…we, we, we
Second Person Plural…	…-tis,-tis,-tis…y'all, y'all, y'all
Third Person Plural…	…-nt, -nt, -nt…they, they, they

WEEK 2: Worksheet   Nomen: _____

Vocabulary: Fill in the missing principal parts in English and in Latin.

amo	amare	amavi	amatum
I love			

canto		cantavi	
	to sing		

			laboratum
I work			

narro			
		I told	

		oravi	
I pray			prayed

Chants: Complete the chants by filling in the empty boxes.

Present Tense Verb Endings

	Singular	Plural
1st Person	-o	
2nd Person		
3rd Person		

English Personal Pronouns

	Singular	Plural
1st Person	I	
2nd Person		
3rd Person		

Grammar: Fill in the blanks with info from your grammar and grammar sound-off.

1. A verb is an _____ or a _____ ___ _____.
2. Every verb has _____ principal parts.
3. The parts are called the Present, _____, _____, Passive Participle or Supine.
4. We get the present _____ from the _____.
5. To get the present stem, _____ off the ___ ___.
6. The _____ is the one doing the verb.
7. The Number can be Singular or _____.

Matching: Draw a straight line matching the Person and Number to the correct Latin ending.

First Person Singular   -mus

Second Person Singular   -tis

Third Person Singular   -o

First Person Plural   -t

Second Person Plural   -nt

Third Person Plural   -s

Word Hunt: Choose the best word from the box to put in each of the sentences below.

| amo | canto | laboro | narro | oro |

1. At church, _____ songs to God.
2. On the farm, _____ in the fields.
3. _____ my friends and family very much.
4. Before bedtime, _____ stories to my sister.
5. _____ to thank God before I eat my lunch.

Matching: Draw a straight line matching the English pronoun to the correct Latin ending.

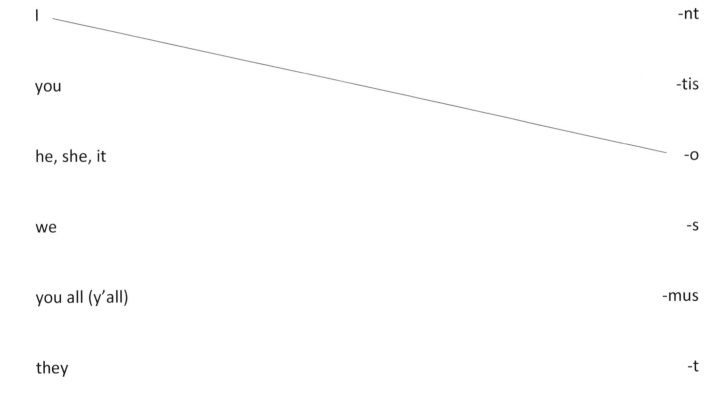

Paideia Latina, Level A | 11

Verb Stems: Chop off the "-re" of the Infinitive (Second Principal Part) to find the present stem for each word.

    amo, ama~~re~~, amavi, amatum → ama-

1. canto, cantare, cantavi, cantatum → _____
2. laboro, laborare, laboravi, laboratum → _____
3. narro, narrare, narravi, narratum → _____
4. oro, orare, oravi, oratum → _____

Derivatives: Use your knowledge of Latin vocabulary to fill in the blanks.

1. The word "laboratory" comes from *laboro*. A laboratory is a place where scientists _____.

2. The word "amorous" comes from *amo*. An amorous person shows lots of _____.

3. The word "cantata" comes from *canto*. A cantata is something that a choir can _____.

4. The word "narration" comes from *narro*. A narration _____ a story.

WEEK 3: Present Tense Verb Translation

Goals: Attach present tense endings to the verb stem and translate the verb.

Vocabulary

ámbulo, ambuláre, ambulávi, ambulátum AHM-boo-loh, ahm-boo-LAH-ray, ahm-boo-LAH-vee, ahm-boo-LAH-toom	I walk, to walk, I walked, walked
do, dáre, dédi, dátum DOH, DAH-ray, DAY-dee, DAH-toom	I give, to give, I gave, given
érro, erráre, errávi, errátum AIR-oh, air-RAH-ray, air-RAH-vee, air-RAH-toom	I wander, to wander, I wandered, wandered
páro, paráre, parávi, parátum PAH-roh, pah-RAH-ray, pah-RAH-vee, pah-RAH-toom	I prepare, to prepare, I prepared, prepared
sto, stáre, stéti, státum STOH, STAH-ray, STAY-tee, STAH-toom	I stand, to stand, I stood, stood
et ET	and
sed SAID	but
non NOHN	not

Chant: Present Tense Verb Amo

	Singular	English	Plural	English
1st Person	amo	I love	amamus	we love
2nd Person	amas	you love	amatis	y'all love
3rd Person	amat	he/she/it loves	amant	they love

Paideia Latina, Level A | 13

Grammar Lesson

In this lesson, we are learning how to attach the present tense verb endings to the verb stem and then how to translate the word. Let's find the stem of "sto, stare, steti, statum":

Infinitive = stare → sta~~re~~ → Stem = sta-

Now we can attach our "-o, -s, -t, -mus, -tis, -nt" endings.

Sta-o → St-o   Sta-mus

Sta-s   Sta-tis

Sta-t   Sta-nt

With the first form, the "a" in the stem is going to disappear. The "o" ending gobbles it up, so instead of "sta-o" we just have "st-o."

To translate, we just look at the ending first and then the stem.

Example: "sta-mus"

(1) The ending is "-mus" so it translates as: "We _____"
(2) The stem means "stand" so it translates: "We stand."

Grammar Sound Off

Review the sound off from last week.

MYTHOLOGY

Jupiter was the king of the Roman gods. His name in Greek was **Zeus**. He ruled earth and heaven from Mount Olympus. As the god of the sky, he hurled lightning bolts at those who displeased him.

WEEK 3: Worksheet   Nomen: _____

Vocabulary: Fill in the missing parts in English and in Latin.

ambulo			ambulatum
		I walked	

	dare	dedi	

erro			
	to wander		

	parare		paratum

sto			
			stood

et	

sed	

non	

Paideia Latina, Level A | 15

Chants: Complete the chants by filling in the empty boxes.

	Singular	English	Plural	English
1st Person	am-o	I love		
2nd Person			ama-tis	
3rd Person				They love

	Singular	English	Plural	English
1st Person	par-o	I prepare		
2nd Person	para-s			
3rd Person			para-nt	

	Singular	English	Plural	English
1st Person	narr-o	I tell		we tell
2nd Person			narra-tis	
3rd Person				

Grammar: Fill in the blanks with info from your grammar and grammar sound-off from this week or from previous weeks.

1. A _____ is an action or a state of being.
2. Each verb has four _____ _____.
3. The parts are called the _____, _____, _____, Passive Participle or Supine.
4. We get the _____ _____ from the Infinitive.
5. To get the present stem, chop off the ____ ____.

Word Hunt: Choose the best word from the box to put in each of the sentences below.

| ambulo | do | erro | paro | sto |

1. If there are not enough chairs for everyone, then _____.
2. _____ presents to my family at Christmas.
3. _____ for my test by studying my Latin vocabulary.
4. I lost my map, so _____ around in the forest.
5. _____ more slowly than I run.

Verb Stems: Chop off the "-re" of the Infinitive (Second Principal Part) to find the present stem for each word.

    ambulo, ambula~~re~~, ambulavi, ambulatum → ambula-

1. do, dare, dedi, datum → _____
2. erro, errare, erravi, erratum → _____
3. paro, parare, paravi, paratum → _____
4. sto, stare, steti, statum → _____

Matching: Draw a straight line matching the English pronoun to the correct Latin ending.

I   -nt

you   -o

he, she, it   -tis

we   -s

you all (y'all)   -t

they   -mus

Translation: Look at the ending, look at the stem, and then translate into English. (Remember that the "-o" ending gobbles up the "a" at the end of the stem.)

    Ambula-mus   We walk.

1. Err-o _____
2. Para-nt _____
3. Sta-s _____
4. Da-tis _____
5. Ama-t _____
6. Labora-nt _____
7. Canta-mus _____
8. Or-o _____
9. Narra-s _____

Story: Read the story below, trying to understand the Latin words mixed in with the English words. (You do not have to write anything down.)

Amo School

Today **ambulo** to school. The other students **ambulant** to school too. To start the day, **cantamus et oramus**. Sometimes the teacher **orat**, **sed** sometimes a student **orat**. The teacher **narrat** a story from our history book **et** asks us questions. After I raise my hand, **sto** up from my chair. **Do** the answer to my teacher. At recess, we play tag **et erramus** around the field. If **non amas** to play tag, you can play on the slide. On Thursday, **paramus** for our tests which will be on Friday. **Laboro** hard at school. **Amo** school.

WEEK 4: Noun Cases; First Declension Noun Endings

Goals: Recite the five noun cases in order, recite the first declension endings, and find the stem of a noun.

Vocabulary

návigo, navigáre, navigávi, navigátum NAH-vee-go, nah-vee-GAH-ray, nah-vee-GAH-vee, nah-vee-GAH-toom	I sail, to sail, I sailed, sailed
áqua, áquae AH-quah, AH-quay	water
cása, cásae CAH-sah, CAH-say	house
discípula, discípulae dis-CHEE-poo-lah, dis-CHEE-poo-lay	female student
fémina, féminae FAY-mee-nah, FAY-mee-nay	woman
ínsula, ínsulae EEN-soo-lah, EEN-soo-lay	island
mágistra, mágistrae MAH-jee-strah, MAH-jee-stray	female teacher
puélla, puéllae pooh-ELL-ah, pooh-ELL-ay	girl
regína, regínae ray-JEE-nah, ray-JEE-nay	queen
sílva, sílvae SEEL-vah, SEEL-vay	forest, woods
térra, térrae TAIR-rah, TAIR-ray	earth, ground, land

Chant: First Declension Feminine Noun Endings

	Singular	Plural
Nominative	-a	-ae
Genitive	-ae	-arum
Dative	-ae	-is
Accusative	-am	-as
Ablative	-ā	-is

Grammar Lesson

A **noun** is a person, place, thing, or idea. In this lesson, we are learning about the five cases for Latin nouns and how to find a noun stem.

A **case** is something that says what *job* a noun is doing in the sentence (subject, direct object, etc.). In English, we use word order to show what job the noun is doing. "The farmer carries the dog" means something very different than "The dog carries the farmer." We know the difference because of the word order. In Latin, the **ending** of the noun tells what job the noun is doing in the sentence. Each of the five cases has its own endings, one for the singular and one for the plural. The five cases in order are: **Nominative, Genitive, Dative, Accusative, and Ablative**. The sentence "**N**o **G**erbils **D**eserve **A**corns, **Ab**by" can help you memorize the cases in order. We will learn later what job each case does.

In your vocabulary list, you are given the Nominative and Genitive singular for each word. In order to find the **noun stem**, go to the second form (the Genitive) and chop off the ending ("-ae")

    Example: femina, femin|ae   Stem = "femin-"

Once you know your noun stem, you can attach all the case endings to it.

Grammar Sound Off

A noun is a person...	...a place, a thing, an idea!
To find the noun stem...	...chop off the Genitive ending.
The case tells you the job...	...the noun does in the sentence.
First case?	Nominative!
Second case?	Genitive!
Third case?	Dative!
Fourth case?	Accusative!
Fifth case?	Ablative!

WEEK 4: Worksheet   Nomen: _____

Vocabulary: Fill in the missing parts in English and in Latin.

navigo			
	to sail		

aqua	aquae	water

casa		

	discipulae	

femina		

insula		

		female teacher

regina		

	puellae	

		forest, woods

	terrae	

Paideia Latina, Level A | 21

Chants: Complete the chants by filling in the empty boxes.

	Singular	English	Plural	English
1st Person	navig-o	I sail		
2nd Person	naviga-s			
3rd Person				

	Singular	English	Plural	English
1st Person	d-o	I give		
2nd Person	da-s			
3rd Person				

First Declension Feminine Noun Endings

	Singular	Plural
Nominative	-a	
Genitive		
Dative		-is
Accusative		
Ablative		

Cases: Write the names of the five cases in order. (Look at the chant above to help spell them correctly!)

1. _____

2. _____

3. _____

4. _____

5. _____

Grammar: Fill in the blanks with info from your grammar and grammar sound-off from this week or from previous weeks.

1. A _____ is an action or a state of being.
2. A _____ is a person, a place, a _____ or an idea.
3. The case tells you the _____ the noun does in the sentence.
4. The first case is _____.
5. The _____ case is Genitive.
6. The third case is _____.
7. The fourth case is _____.
8. The fifth case is _____.
9. To find the _____ _____ chop off the Genitive ending.

Word Hunt: Choose the best word from the box to put in each sentence below.

aqua	casa	discipula	femina	insula
magistra	regina	puella	silva	terra

1. I need a drink of _____.
2. I'm not a boy—I'm a _____!
3. _____ writes the assignment on the whiteboard.
4. The _____ was completely surrounded by water.
5. The _____ wore a crown of gold.
6. The job of the _____ is to learn.
7. You must open the door to enter the _____.
8. The _____ was full of tall trees.
9. A _____ is a girl who is all grown up.
10. The _____ was dry because it had not rained recently.

Paideia Latina, Level A | 23

Noun Stems: Chop off the "-ae" of the Genitive (Second form) to find the noun stem for each word.

    femina, **femin**~~ae~~   →   femin-

1. silva, silvae   →   _____
2. casa, casae   →   _____
3. magistra, magistrae   →   _____
4. puella, puellae   →   _____

Verb Translation: Look at the ending, look at the stem, then translate into English.

(Remember that the "-o" ending gobbles up the "a" at the end of the stem.)

    Sta-mus   We stand.

1. Para-tis   _____
2. Naviga-nt   _____
3. D-o   _____
4. Erra-mus   _____

Story: Read the story below, trying to understand the Latin words mixed in with the English words. (You do not have to write anything down.)

The School on the **Insula**

Femina has a **casa** on a small **insula**. **Femina** is **magistra** at a school. The school is on **terra**—it is not on **insula**. At the **casa** of the **femina** there is a **puella**. **Puella** is a **discipula** at the school. To get to school, **femina et puella navigant** in a boat across the **aqua**. When they reach the **terra**, **ambulant** through a **silva**. While they walk, **femina narrat** a story about a **regina** who used to own this **silva**. **Puella** wants to be **regina** when she grows up. Finally, after their long trip, **stant** in front of the school. "When I am **regina**," says the **puella**, "I will build a school on our **insula** next to our **casa**. In the future, **non navigamus** across the **aqua**. Instead, just **ambulamus** next door."

WEEK 5: Noun Genders; Nominative Case: Subject

Goals: Memorize the three noun genders, attach first declension endings to noun stems, and translate sentences with a subject and verb.

Vocabulary

pórto, portáre, portávi, portátum POR-toh, por-TAH-ray, por-TAH-vee, por-TAH-toom	I carry, to carry, I carried, carried
amíca, amícae (f.) ah-MEE-cah, ah-MEE-chay	female friend
céna, cénae (f.) CHAY-nah, CHAY-nay	meal, dinner
fábula, fábulae (f.) FAH-boo-lah, FAH-boo-lay	story
fília, fíliae (f.) FEE-lee-ah, FEE-lee-ay	daughter
germána, germánae (f.) jer-MAH-nah, jer-MAH-nay	sister
ménsa, ménsae (f.) MEN-sah, MEN-say	table
página, páginae (f.) PAH-jee-nah, PAH-jee-nay	page
sélla, séllae (f.) SELL-ah, SELL-ay	chair
sérva, sérvae (f.) SAIR-vah, SAIR-vay	female slave, female servant
vía, víae (f.) VEE-ah, VEE-ay	road, way, street

Highlight Feminine nouns with pink.

Chant: First Declension Feminine Noun

	Singular	Plural
Nominative	femin-a	femin-ae
Genitive	femin-ae	femin-arum
Dative	femin-ae	femin-is
Accusative	femin-am	femin-as
Ablative	femin-ā	femin-is

Grammar Lesson

In English, words can have three genders: **masculine, feminine, and neuter**. Words like "boy" or "king" or "bull" are masculine. Words like "woman" or "princess" or "mare" are feminine. All other words like "town" or "table" or "horse" are neuter—which means that most nouns in English are neuter.

In Latin nouns have the same three genders. But Latin also assigns "things" and "ideas" that we would consider neuter in English to the masculine or feminine gender. So, for example, the word "table" in Latin is feminine, the word "horse" is masculine, but the word "town" is neuter.

How do you know which gender a word is in Latin? For the first set of Latin words that we learn, there is a simple rule:

> If it ends in "-a" → Feminine
>
> If it ends in "-us" → Masculine
>
> If it ends in "um" → Neuter

The first set of nouns we are learning (last week's and this week's vocabulary) are all **feminine**. The (f.) after the vocabulary tells you it is feminine. These nouns are called First Declension Feminine nouns. A **declension** is a group of nouns that have similar endings. You have already learned the First Declension Feminine chant. When you attach all those endings to the stem of a noun, we call that **declining** the noun.

You have probably already learned that whatever does the verb is called the **subject**. In Latin, the subject of the verb is either contained in the verb's ending (Ama-mus – the subject is the "we" at the end of the verb) or it is a noun in the **Nominative** case. If it is a singular Nominative noun (-a), then the verb should be 3rd person singular ("-t"). If it is a plural Nominative noun (-ae), then the verb should be 3rd person plural ("-nt"). The noun replaces the pronoun *he, she, it* or *they*.

> Example: puell**a** navigat → the girl ~~(she)~~ sails
>
> puell**ae** navigant → the girls ~~(they)~~ sail

Grammar Sound Off

Latin has three genders…	…Masculine, Feminine, Neuter.
Words that end in "-a"…	…are mostly Feminine.
Words that end in "-us"…	…are mostly Masculine.
Words that end in "-um"…	…are mostly Neuter.
To make a subject noun…	…use the Nominative case.
-a, -a, -a in the Singular…	…-ae, -ae, -ae in the Plural.
Subject matches the verb…	…in number—Singular or Plural.
-a, -a, -a with -t…	…-ae, -ae, -ae with -nt

MYTHOLOGY

Juno was the wife of Jupiter. Her name in Greek was **Hera**. She was the goddess of marriage and childbirth and the patron goddess of Rome. In the stories, she is frequently angry at Jupiter for his foolish behavior.

WEEK 5: Worksheet   Nomen: _____

Vocabulary: Fill in the missing parts in English and in Latin.

porto			portatum
	to carry		

amica	amicae	

cena		

		story

filia		

germana		

	mensae	

pagina		

		chair

		female slave, female servant

via		

Chants: Complete the chants by filling in the empty boxes.

	Singular	English	Plural	English
1st Person	port-o	I carry		
2nd Person				
3rd Person				

First Declension Feminine Noun

	Singular	Plural
Nominative	sell-a	

Grammar: Fill in the blanks with info from your grammar and grammar sound-off from this week or from previous weeks.

1. A _____ is an action or a state of being.
2. A _____ is a person, a _____, a thing, or an idea.
3. The _____ tells you the job the noun does in the sentence.
4. The three _____ are: masculine, feminine, and neuter.
5. Words that end in "-a" are mostly _____.
6. Words that end in "-us" are mostly _____.
7. Words that end in "um" are mostly _____.
8. Subject nouns use the _____ case.
9. The First Declension Nominative ending is "-a" in singular and _____ in plural.

Noun Stems: Chop off the "-ae" of the Genitive (Second form) to find the noun stem for each word.

> femina, femin**ae** → femin-
>
> 1. pagina, paginae → _____
>
> 2. mensa, mensae → _____

Nominatives: Change each Nominative Singular to Nominative Plural and translate the plural into English!

> amica → amic*ae* (pl.) → female friend**s**
>
> 1. cena (sg.) → _____ (pl.) → _____
>
> 2. germana (sg.) → _____ (pl.) → _____
>
> 3. filia (sg.) → _____ (pl.) → _____
>
> 4. fabula (sg.) → _____ (pl.) → _____

Word Hunt: Choose the best word from the box for each blank.

amica	cena	fabula	filia	germana
mensa	pagina	sella	serva	via

1. The _____ works hard for her Roman masters.

2. Sit down in this _____.

3. Are you on the correct _____ in this book?

4. The _____ was narrow and full of potholes.

5. The _____ was delicious!

6. The mother asked her _____ to clean her room.

7. I share a room with my _____.

8. The _____ he told me was full of adventure.

9. The _____ was covered with crumbs.

10. My _____ comes over for a play date.

Translation: Translate each sentence into Latin.

EXAMPLE: The woman sings.	
__femin-a__	__canta-t__
Nom/Sg	Verb Stem + 3rd/Sg Ending

1. The daughter loves.

   _____   _____
   Nom/Sg   Verb Stem + 3rd/Sg Ending

2. The sister walks.

   _____   _____
   Nom/Sg   Verb Stem + 3rd/Sg Ending

3. The girls sail.

   _____   _____
   Nom/**Pl**   Verb Stem + 3rd/**Pl** Ending

4. The queens pray.

   _____   _____
   Nom/**Pl**   Verb Stem + 3rd/**Pl** Ending

Fabula: Read the story below, trying to understand the Latin words mixed in with the English words. (You do not have to write anything down.)

Julia's New **Amica**

Julia is a Roman **puella**. She is the **filia** of a rich Roman **femina**. She lives in a big **casa**, but she has no **germana** to play with. She has no **amica** to tell her a **fabula**. Flavia is **serva** in Julia's **casa**. Flavia **portat** the **cena** to the **mensa**. Flavia does not sit in a **sella**. Flavia **stat** by the **mensa** and **dat aqua** to Julia and the rich Roman **femina**. Flavia **laborat** hard. Julia wants Flavia to be her **amica**. "Will you play with me?" she asks. **Sed serva** has too much to do. **Serva** must **portat** away the leftover **cena**. **Serva** must clean the **mensa**. "I will help you clean," said Julia. Julia **laborat** hard. Now Flavia has time to play. Flavia tells Julia a **fabula**. Flavia is Julia's new **amica**.

WEEK 6: REVIEW

Goals: Retain and recall vocabulary and grammar from weeks 2-5.

Vocabulary

Check off the ones you know.

- ☐ **ambulo** — I walk
- ☐ **amica** — female friend
- ☐ **amo** — I love
- ☐ **aqua** — water
- ☐ **canto** — I sing
- ☐ **casa** — house
- ☐ **cena** — dinner, meal
- ☐ **discipula** — female student
- ☐ **do** — I give
- ☐ **erro** — I wander
- ☐ **et** — and
- ☐ **fabula** — story
- ☐ **femina** — woman
- ☐ **filia** — daughter
- ☐ **germana** — sister
- ☐ **insula** — island
- ☐ **laboro** — I work
- ☐ **magistra** — female teacher
- ☐ **mensa** — table
- ☐ **narro** — I tell
- ☐ **navigo** — I sail
- ☐ **non** — not
- ☐ **oro** — I pray
- ☐ **pagina** — page
- ☐ **paro** — I prepare
- ☐ **porto** — I carry
- ☐ **puella** — girl
- ☐ **regina** — queen
- ☐ **sed** — but
- ☐ **sella** — chair
- ☐ **serva** — female slave/servant
- ☐ **silva** — forest, woods
- ☐ **sto** — I stand
- ☐ **terra** — earth, ground, land
- ☐ **via** — road, way, street

MYTHOLOGY

Ceres was the Roman goddess of grain and of growing things. Her Greek name was **Demeter**. We get the word "cereal" from her Roman name.

WEEK 6: Review Worksheet   Nomen: _____

Chant: Fill in the blanks for this First Declension Feminine Noun.

	Singular	Plural
	pagin-a	
Dative		

Matching Ricochet: Draw a straight line to match the Person/Number to the verb ending, and then match the verb ending to the English translation.

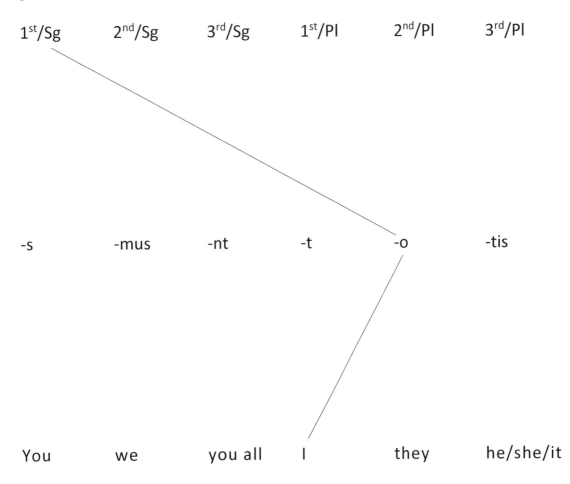

Paideia Latina, Level A | 33

Vocabulary: Fill in the crossword puzzle with vocabulary words from chapters 2-5.

Word Bank

AMBULO	AMICA	AMO	AQUA	CANTO	CASA	CENA	DISCIPULA	DO	ERRO	ET
FABULA	FEMINA	FILIA	GERMANA	INSULA	LABORO	MAGISTRA	MENSA	NARRO
NAVIGO	NON	ORO	PAGINA	PARO	PORTO	PUELLA	REGINA	SED	SELLA	SERVA
SILVA	STO	TERRA	VIA

Across

4. but
5. I prepare
8. dinner
10. female teacher
12. not
14. female student
16. road, way, street
17. I walk
18. house
20. I pray
22. I wander
24. page
26. forest, woods
27. table
29. female slave, female servant
30. I stand
31. I sing
32. chair

Down

1. earth, ground, land
2. daughter
3. I give
5. girl
6. woman
7. story
9. and
11. island
12. I tell
13. I sail
15. I work
19. water
21. queen
23. sister
24. I carry
25. I love
28. female friend

Chant: Fill in the blanks of this present tense verb.

	Singular	English	Plural	English
1st Person	or-o	I pray		
2nd Person				
3rd Person				

Translation: Translate these sentences into English.

1. Navigatis.

2. Oro sed laboras.

3. Magistra ambulat.

4. Magistrae ambulant.

5. Serva cantat.

6. Servae cantant.

7. Erramus in* silvā.

8. Germanae stant in casā.

> *The Latin word "in" means "in" or "on" in English. It is a kind of word called a **preposition**. You will learn later that "in" goes with the Ablative case (which is why the word following it has a line over the ending), but don't worry about that for right now—just translate it as "in"!

Derivatives: On the boxes in the branches of each tree, write English words that come from the Latin root at the bottom of the tree.

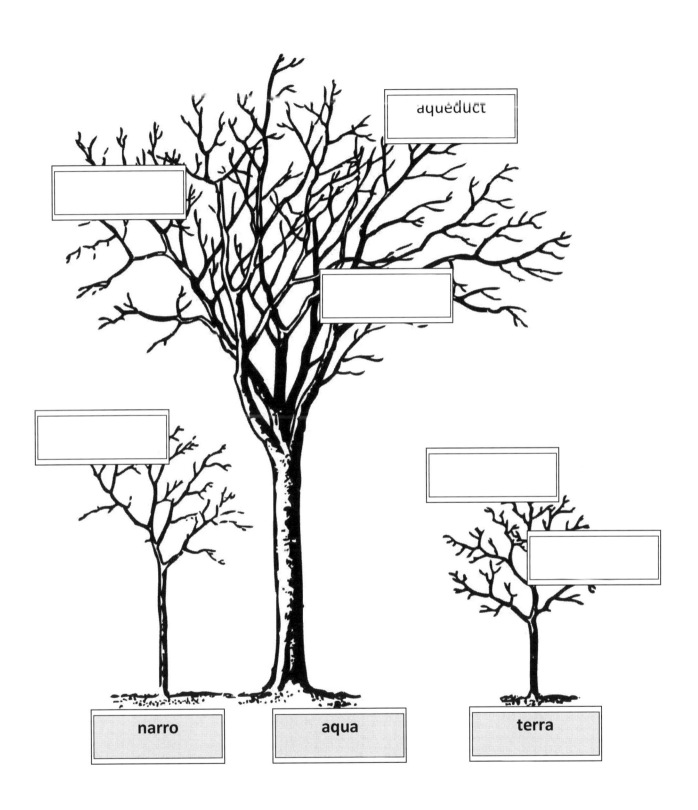

WEEK 7: Second Declension Masculine Noun Endings

Goals: Recite the second declension masculine endings and attach them to a noun.

Vocabulary

rógo, rogáre, rogávi, rogátum ROH-go, roh-GAH-ray, roh-GAH-vee, roh-GAH-toom	I ask, to ask, I asked, asked
amícus, amíci (m.) uh-MEE-coose, uh-MEE-chee	male friend
discípulus, discípuli (m.) dis-CHEE-poo-loose, dis-CHEE-poo-lee	male student
fílius, fílii (m.) FEE-lee-oose, FEE-lee-ee	son
flúvius, flúvii (m.) FLU-vee-oose, FLU-vee-ee	river
germánus, germáni (m.) jer-MAH-noose, jer-MAH-nee	brother
lúpus, lúpi (m.) LOO-poose, LOO-pee	wolf
mágister, mágistri (m.) MAH-jee-stir, MAH-jee-stree	male teacher
púer, púeri (m.) POO-air, POO-air-ee	boy
sérvus, sérvi (m.) SAIR-voose, SAIR-vee	male slave, male servant
vír, víri (m.) VEER, VEER-ee	man

Highlight Masculine nouns with blue.

Chant: Second Declension Masculine Noun Endings

	Singular	Plural
Nominative	-us / r	-i
Genitive	-i	-orum
Dative	-o	-is
Accusative	-um	-os
Ablative	-o	-is

Chant: Second Declension Masculine Noun

	Singular	Plural
Nominative	serv-us	serv-i
Genitive	serv-i	serv-orum
Dative	serv-o	serv-is
Accusative	serv-um	serv-os
Ablative	serv-o	serv-is

Grammar Lesson

The **second declension** is made up of masculine nouns that end in -us or -r and neuter nouns that end in -um. In this lesson, we will focus on the masculine nouns. All of your masculine nouns are marked with an (m.) in the list.

In your vocabulary list, you are given the Nominative and Genitive singular for each word. In order to find the **noun stem**, go to the second form (the Genitive) and chop off the ending ("-i")

    Example: lupus, lup~~i~~   Stem = "lup-"

    Puer, puer~~i~~   Stem = "puer-"

Remember that when we want to use a noun as the subject, it should be in the **Nominative** case. If it is a singular Nominative noun ("-us / -r"), then the verb should be 3rd person singular ("-t"). If it is a plural Nominative noun ("-i"), then the verb should be 3rd person plural ("-nt").

    Example: puer rogat → the boy asks

                      pueri rogant → the boys ask

Grammar Sound Off

Latin has three genders…	…Masculine, Feminine, Neuter.
Words that end in "-a"…	…are mostly Feminine.
Words that end in "-us"…	…are mostly Masculine.
Words that end in "-um"…	…are mostly Neuter.
To make a subject noun…	…use the Nominative case.
-a, -a, -a in the Singular…	…-ae, -ae, -ae in the Plural.
-us, -us, -us in the Singular…	**…-i, -i, -i in the Plural.**
Subject matches the verb…	…in number—Singular or Plural.
-a, -a, -a with -t…	…-ae, -ae, -ae with -nt
-us, -us, -us with -t…	**…-i, -i, -i with -nt**

MYTHOLOGY

Neptune and **Pluto** were Jupiter's brothers. Neptune, whose Greek name was **Poseidon** was the god of the sea. Pluto, whose Greek name was **Hades,** was the god of the underworld.

WEEK 7: Worksheet   Nomen: _____

Vocabulary: Fill in the missing parts in English and in Latin.

rogo			
		I asked	

amicus	amici	

discipulus		

		son

		river

germanus		

	lupi	

magister		

		boy

		male slave, male servant

vir		

Chants: Complete the chants by filling in the empty boxes.

	Singular	English	Plural	English
1st Person		I ask		
2nd Person				
3rd Person	roga-t			

Second Declension Masculine Noun Endings

	Singular	Plural
	-us	
Genitive		

Second Declension Masculine Noun

	Singular	Plural
	lup-us	
Dative		

Grammar: Fill in the blanks with info from your grammar and grammar sound-off from this week or from previous weeks.

1. The _____ tells you the job the noun does in the sentence.
2. Subject nouns use the _____ case.
3. The First Declension Nominative ending is "-a" in singular and _____ in plural.
4. The Second Declension Masculine Nominative ending is "-us" in singular and _____ in plural.
5. Words that end in "-a" are mostly _____.
6. Words that end in "-us" are mostly _____.
7. Words that end in "um" are mostly _____.

Noun Stems: Chop off the "-i" of the Genitive (Second form) to find the noun stem for each word.

lupus, **lupi** → lup-

1. puer, pueri → _____
2. amicus, amici → _____
3. germanus, germani → _____
4. vir, viri → _____
5. magister, magistri → _____

Nominatives: Change each Nominative Singular to Nominative Plural and translate the plural into English!

amicus → amic*i* (pl.) → male friend*s*

1. servus (sg.) → _____ (pl.) → _____
2. vir (sg.) → _____ (pl.) → _____
3. filius (sg.) → _____ (pl.) → _____
4. puer (sg.) → _____ (pl.) → _____

Word Hunt: Choose the <u>best</u> word from the box for each blank.

amicus	discipulus	filius	fluvius	germanus
lupus	magister	puer	servus	vir

1. The _____ does his homework.
2. The bridge goes across the _____.
3. The _____ will attack the sheep.
4. My sister and _____ are younger than me.
5. The _____ writes the assignment on the whiteboard.
6. The cruel Roman master beats his _____.
7. I made a new _____ today.
8. They bought blue clothes since the new baby was a _____.
9. "My _____, hear the instruction of your father."
10. The soldier was a brave _____.

Fabula: Read the story below, trying to understand the Latin words mixed in with the English words. (You do not have to write anything down.)

The Dangerous **Lupus**

One day, a **discipulus ambulat** home from school. The **discipulus** crosses a **fluvius et errat** in the **silva**. The father of the **discipulus** had warned him never to go in the **silva** alone. "Why?" the **discipulus rogat**. His father **non narrat** him. "One day, when you are a **vir**, my **filius**, then you can go there." **Sed** today, the **puer** has left his school, **et** his **magister**, **et** all his **amici**, **et** disobeyed his father. He does not have a **germanus** or even a **servus** to go with him. The deep, dark **silva** is full of trees, and behind the trees is hiding a **lupus**. The **lupus amat** to eat little **pueri et puellae**. The **lupus** follows the **discipulus** with silent steps, eager for this new **cena**. The **puer** is lost **et stat** beneath a tree and cries. **Lupus** is just about to spring on the **puer**, when suddenly, a spear flies through the air and hits the **lupus**. A **vir** has come to look for the **discipulus**. "My **filius**," says the **vir**, "now you know why you are never **ambulare** in the **silva** alone. Now come, help me **portare** this **lupus**. He wanted to make you his **cena**, but we will make him ours."

WEEK 8: Irregular Verb "Sum"; Second Declension Masculine Continued

Goals: Recite the present tense of "sum" in Latin and English and use second declension masculine nouns in a sentence.

Vocabulary

súm, ésse, fúi, futúrum SOOM, ES-say, FOO-ee, foo-TOO-room	I am, to be, I was, about to be
aquárius, aquárii (m.) ah-QUAH-ree-oose, ah-QUAH-ree-ee	water-carrier
cámelus, cámeli (m.) CAH-meh-loose, CAH-meh-lee	camel
Chrístus, Chrísti (m.) CREE-stoose, CREE-stee	Christ
cíbus, cíbi (m.) CHEE-boose, CHEE-bee	food
déus, déi (m.) DAY-oose, DAY-ee	god
dóminus, dómini (m.) DOH-mee-noose, DOH-mee-nee	lord, master
elephántus, elephánti (m.) ay-lay-FON-toose, ay-lay-FON-tee	elephant
équus, équi (m.) AY-kwoose, AY-kwee	horse
lúdus, lúdi (m.) LOO-doose, LOO-dee	school, game
stílus, stíli (m.) STEE-loose, STEE-lee	stylus, pen

Highlight Masculine nouns with blue.

Chant: Present Tense Verb Sum

	Singular	**English**	**Plural**	**English**
1st Person	sum	I am	sumus	we are
2nd Person	es	you are	estis	you all are
3rd Person	est	he/she/it is	sunt	they are

Grammar Lesson

Remember when we said that a **verb** can be an action or a state of being? We have been learning action verbs up until now, but this week we are learning our first "state of being" verb. It is called a **linking verb**. It connects two things together by saying that one of them *is* the other one. You can think of it as an equal sign (=).

    Example: My teacher *is* a woman.

This verb, "sum, esse, fui, futurum" is an **irregular verb**. This means that instead of all four parts having similar stems, they have very different stems. Normally, we can find our verb stem by chopping the "-re" off the infinitive (the second principal part), but with this verb, we have two stems: "su-" and "es-" which each get three forms of the chant. We can add our verb endings to these stems, but there are a couple of changes. Instead of "-o" for the first person singular, we use "-m." And the second person singular "-s" gets swallowed up by the "s" that is already there at the end of the stem.

su-m	**su**-mus
es	**es**-tis
es-t	**su**-nt

Grammar Sound Off

Irregular verbs…	…don't have regular stems.
What is the person?	The one doing the verb!
What is the number?	Singular or Plural!
First Person Singular…	…-o or -m…I, I, I
Second Person Singular…	…-s,-s,-s…you, you, you
Third Person Singular…	…-t,-t,-t…he, she, it
First Person Plural…	…-mus,-mus,-mus…we, we, we
Second Person Plural…	…-tis,-tis,-tis…y'all, y'all, y'all
Third Person Plural…	…-nt, -nt, -nt…they, they, they

WEEK 8: Worksheet Nomen: _____

Vocabulary: Fill in the missing parts in English and in Latin.

| sum | | | |
| | | | about to be |

| aquarius | aquarii | |

| camelus | | |

| | | Christ |

| | cibi | |

| deus | | |

| | domini | |

| elephantus | | |

| | | horse |

| | | school, game, play |

| stilus | | |

Paideia Latina, Level A | 47

Chants: Complete the chants by filling in the empty boxes.

	Singular	English	Plural	English
1st Person	sum	I am		
2nd Person				
3rd Person				

First Declension Feminine Noun

	Singular	Plural
	terr-a	
Genitive		

Second Declension Masculine Noun

	Singular	Plural
Nominative	camel-us	

Chant Questions: Answer the questions about chant endings.

1. What is the Nom/Sg/Masc ending? ____-us____
2. What is the Nom/Pl/Masc ending? _____
3. What is the Nom/Sg/Fem ending? _____
4. What is the Nom/Pl/Fem ending? _____
5. What is the 3rd/Sg verb ending? _____
6. What is the 3rd/Pl verb ending? _____

Grammar: Fill in the blanks with info from your grammar and grammar sound-off from this week or from previous weeks.

1. A _____ is an action or a state of being.
2. Each verb has four _____ _____.
3. The parts are called the _____, _____ _____ , _____, Passive Participle or Supine.
4. We get the _____ _____ from the Infinitive.
5. To get the present stem, chop off the ____ ____.
6. Irregular verbs don't have _____ stems.

Noun Stems: Chop off the ending of the Genitive (second form) to find the noun stem for each word.

lupus, **lupi** → lup-

1. terra, terrae → _____
2. elephantus, elephanti → _____
3. equus, equi → _____
4. sella, sellae → _____
5. magister, magistri → _____

Matching: Draw a straight line to match the Latin to the English.

Sum — You are
Es — I am
Est   You all are
Sumus   He/she/it is
Estis   They are
Sunt   We are

Paideia Latina, Level A | 49

Word Hunt: Choose the <u>best</u> word from the box for each blank.

aquarius	camelus	cibus	Christus	deus
dominus	elephantus	equus	ludus	stylus

1. The _____ has one or two humps, and the _____ has a trunk.
2. _____ is the Son of _____.
3. At _____, I use my _____ on my tablet.
4. The _____ brought two buckets.
5. A _____ rides an _____ while a slave walks.
6. I'm starving! I need _____.

Translation: Translate each sentence <u>into Latin</u>.

EXAMPLE: The elephant walks.		The elephants walk.	
__elephant-us__	__ambula-t__	__elephant-i__	__ambula-nt__
Nom/Sg/Masc	Verb Stem + 3rd/Sg Ending	Nom/Pl/Masc.	Verb Stem + 3rd/Pl

1. The water-carrier works.

   _____ _____
   Nom/Sg/Masc   Verb Stem + 3rd/Sg

2. The water-carriers work.

   _____ _____
   Nom/**Pl**/Masc   Verb Stem + 3rd/**Pl**

3. The boy asks.

   _____ _____
   Nom/Sg/Masc   Verb Stem + 3rd/Sg

4. The boys ask.

   _____ _____
   Nom/**Pl**/Masc   Verb Stem + 3rd/**Pl**

5. The woman prays.

   _____ _____
   Nom/Sg/**Fem**   Verb Stem + 3rd/Sg

6. The women pray.

   _____ _____
   Nom/**Pl**/**Fem**   Verb Stem + 3rd/**Pl**

Derivatives: Give an English derivative for each Latin root.

1. The word "amicable" comes from *amicus*. If someone is amicable, then they are _____ to you.

2. Jupiter and Juno were Roman deities. The word "deity" comes from *deus* and is another way of saying _____.

3. The word "equestrian" comes from *equus*. An equestrian is someone who rides a _____.

4. The word "dominion" comes from the word *dominus*. To take dominion over a piece of land is to be the _____ of it.

5. Sailors figure out what direction to sail by _____, a word that comes from *navigo*.

Fabula: Read the story below, trying to understand the Latin words mixed in with the English words. (You do not have to write anything down.)

The Amazing Camelus

Cameli are funny creatures. **Christus**, the **Filius** of **Deus**, said that **est** easier for a **camelus** to go through the eye of a needle than it is for a rich **vir** to enter the kingdom of **Deus**. **Cameli sunt** famous for being able to hold lots of **aqua**. **Cameli** can go for three days in the desert without **aqua** or **cibus**. They can last much longer than the **elephantus** or the **equus**. The camelus itself **est** an **aquarius**. It stores **aqua** and **cibus** inside its humps. **Cameli** are fun to draw. On the bottom of this **pagina**, try drawing a **camelus** with your **stilus**. See who can draw the best **camelus** in the whole **ludus**!

WEEK 9: Nominative Case: Predicate Nominative

*Goals: Identify Subject Nouns and Predicate Nominatives
and use forms of "sum" in a sentence.*

Vocabulary

fló, fláre, flávi, flátum FLOW, FLAH-ray, FLAH-vee, FLAH-toom	I blow, to blow, I blew, blown
áger, ágri (m.) AH-jer, AH-gree	field (for farming)
cámpus, cámpi (m.) CAHM-poose, CAHM-pee	field, level space, plain
hérba, hérbae (f.) HAIR-bah, HAIR-bay	herb, grass, plant
hórtus, hórti (m.) HOR-toose, HOR-tee	garden
íra, írae (f.) EE-rah, EE-ray	anger
lócus, lóci (m.) LOH-coose, LOH-chee	place
pátria, pátriae (f.) PAH-tree-ah, PAH-tree-ay	fatherland, country
rósa, rósae (f.) ROH-sah, ROH-say	rose
úrsa, úrsae (f.) ER-sah, ER-say	bear (the animal)
véntus, vénti (m.) VEN-toose, VEN-tee	wind

Highlight Masculine nouns with Blue, Feminine nouns with Pink.

Grammar Lesson

This week we will look at how to use "sum, esse, fui, futurum" in a sentence. When we connect two nouns with this **linking verb** (LV), the first noun is the **subject noun** (SN). The second noun is called the **predicate Nominative** (PRN). The predicate Nominative renames the subject.

    SN   LV   PRN
    Magistra est femina.
    The teacher is a woman.

In Latin, when we have a **subject pronoun** (SP), the subject is usually included in the verb.

    SP/LV   PRN   SP/LV PRN
    Sum discipulus.   **Es vir.**
    I am a student.   You are a man.

The predicate Nominative needs to agree with the subject in case and number. So, if the subject is a plural Nominative, the predicate Nominative should be a plural Nominative. (And the verb should be a plural verb!)

    SN   LV   PRN   SP/LV   PRN
    Filiae sunt puellae.   **Estis elephanti.**
    The daughters are girls.   You all are elephants.

Grammar Sound Off

Nominative case...   ...Subject Noun, S-N, Predicate Nominative, P-R-N

The Subject Noun...   ...does the verb.

The Predicate Nominative...   ...renames the subject.

They're connected...   ...by a linking verb.

SN-LV-PRN...   ...SN-LV-PRN

MYTHOLOGY

Mars was the Roman god of war and his Greek name was **Ares**. He was the son of Jupiter and Juno. He was also the father of Romulus, the founder of the war-like city of Rome.

Paideia Latina, Level A | 53

WEEK 9: Worksheet   Nomen: _____

Vocabulary: Fill in the missing parts in English and in Latin.

flo			
I blow		I blew	

| ager | agri | m. | |

| campus | | | |

| herba | | f. | |

| | horti | | |

| | | | anger |

| | | | place |

| patria | | | |

| rosa | | | |

| | | | bear (the animal) |

| ventus | | | |

54 | Paideia Latina, Level A

Chants: Complete the chants by filling in the empty boxes.

	Singular	English	Plural	English
1st Person	sum	I am		
2nd Person				
3rd Person				

	Singular	English	Plural	English
1st Person		I blow		
2nd Person	fla-s			
3rd Person				

Word Hunt: Choose the best word from the box for each blank.

ager	campus	herba	hortus	ira
locus	patria	rosa	ursa	ventus

1. The farmer plows the _____.
2. I picked a red _____ out of the _____.
3. The _____ blows.
4. You need to find a _____ to store your colored pencils.
5. His face was full of _____.
6. In my _____, we vote to elect a president.
7. Never get between a mother _____ and her cubs!
8. Long green _____ covered the large _____.

Grammar: Fill in the blanks with info from your grammar and grammar sound-off from this week or from previous weeks.

1. A _____ is a person, place, thing, or _____.
2. The _____ case is for Subject Nouns & Predicate Nominatives.
3. The Subject Noun _____ the verb.
4. The Predicate Nominative _____ the subject.
5. We connect the SN and the PRN with a _____ verb.

Plurals: Make each Nominative noun plural.

camelus → cameli

1. rosa → _____
2. hortus → _____
3. casa → _____
4. locus → _____
5. ursa → _____
6. patria → _____

Labeling and Translating: Label with one set of these abbreviations and translate.

| SN LV PRN | SP/LV PRN |

SN LV PRN
Locus est campus. → The place is a field.

___ ___ ___
1. Rosa est herba. → _____

___ ___ ___
2. Feminae sunt magistrae. → _____

___ ___
3. Sumus discipuli. → _____

___ ___
4. Estis aquarii. → _____

Derivatives: On the boxes in the branches of each tree, write English words that come from the Latin root at the bottom of the tree.

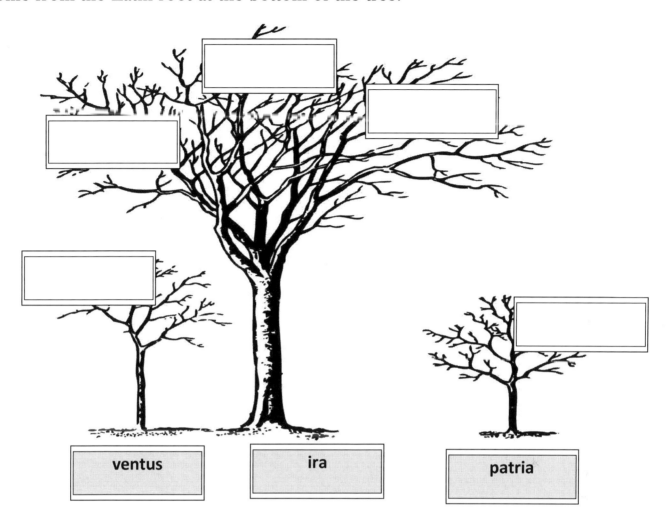

Fabula: Read the story below, trying to understand the Latin words mixed in with the English words. (You do not have to write anything down.)

The **Ursa** in the **Hortus**

Once upon a time in the **patria** of **Italia**, **puella ambulat** outside her **casa** and through the **ager** to her **hortus**. **Hortus est** full of **herbae**. **Puella** pours **aqua** on the **herbae et** picks a red **rosa** off a bush. Nearby **hortus est campus et** nearby **campus est silva**. A large **ursa** lives in **silva**. **Non est cibus in silva et ursa ambulat** across **campus** to **hortus** of **puella**. **Ursa amat** berries **et sunt** berries in **hortus**. When **puella ambulat** to the last row of **hortus**, she sees **ursa** eating her berries. "Shoo! Shoo!" **puella narrat ursa** with **ira** in her voice. **Ursa est** big, **sed puella est** brave. **Ursa dat puella** a small growl, **et ambulat** away to find more berries somewhere else.

WEEK 10: Second Declension Neuter Noun Endings

Goals: Recite the second declension neuter endings and attach them to a noun.

Vocabulary

íntro, intráre, intrávi, intrátum EEN-troh, een-TRAH-ray, een-TRAH-vee, een-TRAH-toom	I enter, to enter, I entered, entered
aedifícium, aedifícii (n.) ay-dee-FEE-chee-oom, ay-dee-FEE-chee-ee	building
béllum, bélli (n.) BEL-loom, BEL-lee	war
cáelum, cáeli (n.) CHAY-loom, CHAY-lee	sky, heaven
cástellum, cástelli (n.) CAHS-tel-loom, CAHS-tel-lee	castle, fortress
dónum, dóni (n.) DOH-noom, DOH-nee	gift
frúmentum, frúmenti (n.) FROO-men-toom, FROO-men-tee	grain
fórum, fóri (n.) FOH-room, FOH-ree	marketplace
óppidum, óppidi (n.) OH-pee-doom, OH-pee-dee	town
témplum, témpli (n.) TEM-ploom, TEM-plee	temple
vínum, víni (n.) VEE-noom, VEE-nee	wine

Highlight Neuter nouns with yellow.

Chant: Second Declension Neuter Noun Endings

	Singular	Plural
Nominative	-um	-a
Genitive	-i	-orum
Dative	-o	-is
Accusative	-um	-a
Ablative	-o	-is

Chant: Second Declension Neuter Noun

	Singular	Plural
Nominative	bell-um	bell-a
Genitive	bell-i	bell-orum
Dative	bell-o	bell-is
Accusative	bell-um	bell-a
Ablative	bell-o	bell-is

Grammar Lesson

The **second declension** is made up of masculine nouns that end in -us or -r and neuter nouns that end in -um. In this lesson, we will focus on the neuter nouns. All of your neuter nouns are marked with an (n.) in the list.

The neuter chant is very similar to the masculine chant. The three differences are: (1) the Nominative singular is "-um," (2) the Nominative plural is "-a," and (3) the Accusative Plural is "-a." Notice that the Nominative and Accusative match each other in both the singular and the plural. This is part of what is known as the neuter rule. The **neuter rule** states that the Nominative and Accusative will always match and that there will always be an "-a" in the plural ending.

Grammar Sound Off

Latin has three genders...	...Masculine, Feminine, Neuter.
Words that end in "-a"...	...are mostly Feminine.
Words that end in "-us"...	...are mostly Masculine.
Words that end in "-um"...	...are mostly Neuter.
Nominative case...	...Subject Noun, SN. Predicate Nominative, PRN.
The Subject Noun...	...does the verb.
The Predicate Nominative...	...renames the subject.
They're connected...	...by a small L-V.
SN-LV-PRN...	...SN-LV-PRN
-a, -a, -a in the Singular...	...-ae, -ae, -ae in the Plural.
-us, -us, -us in the Singular...	...-i, -i, -i in the Plural.
-um, -um, -um in the Singular...	**...-a, -a, -a in the Plural.**
Subject matches the verb...	...in number—Singular or Plural.
-a, -a, -a with -t...	...-ae, -ae, -ae with -nt
-us, -us, -us with -t...	...-i, -i, -i with -nt
-um, -um, -um with -t...	**...-a, -a, -a with -nt**
The neuter rule states...	**...the Nominative matches the Accusative,**
And in the plural those cases...	**...always have an A.**

MYTHOLOGY

Venus was the Roman goddess of love and beauty. Her Greek name was **Aphrodite**. After the Trojan War, she helped her human son Aeneas escape burning Troy and flee to Italy. The story is told in the *Aeneid*.

WEEK 10: Worksheet   Nomen: _____

Vocabulary: Fill in the missing parts in English and in Latin.

intro			intratum
I enter			

| aedificium | aedificii | n. | |

| bellum | | | |

| caelum | | n. | |

| | castelli | | |

| | | | gift |

| | | | grain |

| forum | | | |

| | oppidi | | |

| | templi | | |

| | | | wine |

Paideia Latina, Level A | 61

Chants: Complete the chants by filling in the empty boxes.

	Singular	English	Plural	English
1st Person			intra-mus	we enter
2nd Person				
3rd Person				

Second Declension Neuter Noun Endings

	Singular	Plural
Nominative	-um	

Second Declension Neuter Noun

	Singular	Plural
	castell-um	
Dative		

Chant Questions: Answer the questions about chant endings.

1. What is the Nom/Sg/Neut ending? __-um__
2. What is the Nom/Pl/Neut ending? _____
3. What is the 3rd/Sg verb ending? _____
4. What is the 3rd/Pl verb ending? _____

Grammar: Fill in the blanks with info from your grammar and grammar sound-off from this week or from previous weeks.

1. The _____ case is for Subject Nouns & Predicate Nominatives.
2. The Subject Noun _____ the verb.
3. The Predicate Nominative _____ the subject.
4. We connect the SN and the PRN with a _____ verb.
5. The neuter rule states the _____ matches the _____, and in the plural those cases always have an _____.

Plurals: Make each Nominative noun plural and translate into English.

castellum → castella = castles

1. bellum → _____ = _____
2. aedificium → _____ = _____
3. oppidum → _____ = _____
4. donum → _____ = _____

Word Hunt: Choose the best word from the box for each blank.

| aedificium | bellum | caelum | castellum | donum |
| frumentum | forum | oppidum | templum | vinum |

1. To what **aedificium** does a Roman go to offer a sacrifice? _____
2. What does a Roman make out of grapes? _____
3. What do the enemy besiege during a **bellum**? _____
4. What does a farmer grow in his **ager**? _____
5. Where in **oppidum** does the farmer go to sell his produce? _____
6. What do you get for your birthday? _____
7. Where do birds fly? _____

Matching: Draw straight lines (with a ruler!) to match up the neuter nouns with their translations. Watch out for Singular ("-um") and Plural ("-a").

Aedificium		War
Bellum		Gift
Dona		Building
Aedificia		Grain
Frumentum		Wine
Donum		Sky
Bella		Castle
Templa		Marketplace
Vinum		Wars
Oppida		Gifts
Caela		Buildings
Vina		Temples
Castellum		Towns
Forum		Wines
Fora		Skies
Caelum		Marketplaces

Fabula: Read the story below, trying to understand the Latin words mixed in with the English words. (You do not have to write anything down.)

At the **Forum**

The **caelum est** full of **aqua** on the day **intramus oppidum**. In our wagon **portamus** barrels of **vinum** that we made from the grapes in our **ager**. **Portamus** sheafs of **frumentum**. The first **aedificium** we pass **est templum**. **Est templum** of Mars, **deus** of **bellum**. **Damus** the priests a little **vinum** and **frumentum** as **donum**. On the hill above **oppidum** is another **aedificium**, **castellum**. If **bellum** begins, all **viri, feminae, pueri, et puellae** from **oppidum** will go into **castellum** for protection. Now **sumus** at **forum**. **Est** still much **aqua** in **caelum**, much **aqua** on our wagon, **et** much **aqua** on us! We unload **frumentum et vinum**. This time **non damus cibum** as **donum**. **Sumus** here to make money at **forum**.

WEEK 11: REVIEW

Goals: Retain and recall vocabulary and grammar from weeks 7-10.

Vocabulary

Check off the ones you know.

- ☐ **aedificium** — building
- ☐ **ager** — field
- ☐ **amicus** — male friend
- ☐ **aquarius** — water-carrier
- ☐ **bellum** — war
- ☐ **caelum** — sky, heaven
- ☐ **camelus** — camel
- ☐ **campus** — plain, field
- ☐ **castellum** — castle, fortress
- ☐ **Christus** — Christ
- ☐ **cibus** — food
- ☐ **deus** — god
- ☐ **discipulus** — male student
- ☐ **dominus** — lord, master
- ☐ **donum** — gift
- ☐ **elephantus** — elephant
- ☐ **equus** — horse
- ☐ **filius** — son
- ☐ **flo** — I blow
- ☐ **fluvius** — river
- ☐ **forum** — marketplace
- ☐ **frumentum** — grain
- ☐ **germanus** — brother
- ☐ **herba** — herb, grass, plant
- ☐ **hortus** — garden
- ☐ **intro** — I enter
- ☐ **ira** — anger
- ☐ **locus** — place
- ☐ **ludus** — school, game
- ☐ **lupus** — wolf
- ☐ **magister** — male teacher
- ☐ **oppidum** — town
- ☐ **patria** — fatherland, country
- ☐ **puer** — boy
- ☐ **rogo** — I ask
- ☐ **rosa** — rose
- ☐ **servus** — male slave/servant
- ☐ **stilus** — stylus, pen
- ☐ **sum** — I am
- ☐ **templum** — temple
- ☐ **ursa** — bear
- ☐ **ventus** — wind
- ☐ **vinum** — wine
- ☐ **vir** — man

WEEK 11: Review Worksheet

Nomen: _____

Vocabulary: Fill in the crossword with vocabulary words from chapters 7-10.

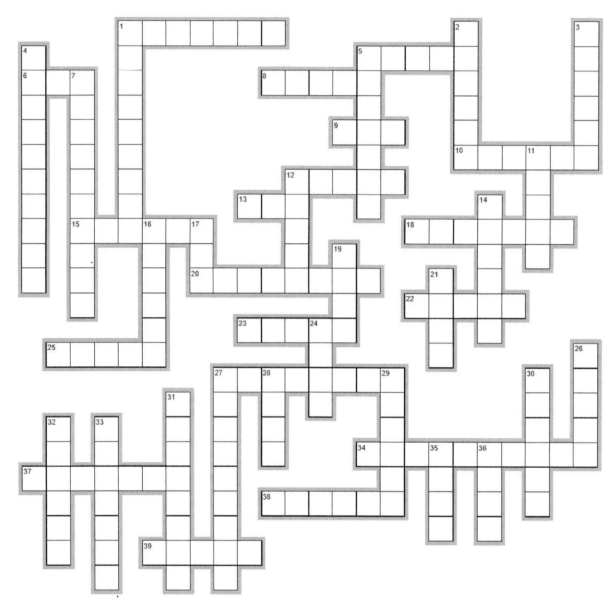

Word Bank

AEDIFICIUM   AGER   AMICUS   BELLUM   CAELUM   CAMELUS   CAMPUS   CASTELLUM
CHRISTUS   CIBUS   DEUS   DISCIPULUS   DOMINUS   DONUM   ELEPHANTUS   EQUUS   FILIUS
FLO   FLUVIUS   FORUM   FRUMENTUM   GERMANUS   HERBA   HORTUS   INTRO   IRA
LOCUS   LUDUS   LUPUS   MAGISTER   OPPIDUM   PATRIA   PUER   ROGO   ROSA   SERVUS
STILUS   SUM   TEMPLUM   URSA   VENTUS   VINUM   VIR

Across

1. river
5. gift
6. anger
8. I enter
9. man
10. male slave/servant
12. school, game
13. I blow
15. plain, field
18. camel
20. male teacher
22. marketplace
23. horse
25. herb, grass, plant
27. Christ
34. elephant
37. temple
38. son
39. wolf

Down

1. grain
2. male friend
3. garden
4. male student
5. lord, master
7. building
11. wine
12. place
14. war
16. fatherland, country
17. I am
19. god
21. I ask
24. bear
26. food
27. castle, fortress
28. rose
29. stylus, pen
30. wind
31. brother
32. sky, heaven
33. town
35. boy
36. field (for farming)

Chants: Complete the chants by filling in the empty boxes.

	Singular	English	Plural	English
1st Person		I ask		
2nd Person				
3rd Person	roga-t			

	Singular	English	Plural	English
1st Person	sum	I am		
2nd Person				
3rd Person				

First Declension Feminine Noun

	Singular	Plural
Nom.	herb-a	
Gen.		
Dat.		
Acc.		
Abl.		

Second Declension Neuter Noun

	Singular	Plural
Nom.	bell-um	
Gen.		
Dat.		
Acc.		
Abl.		

Second Declension Masc. Noun

	Singular	Plural
Nom.	equ-us	
Gen.		
Dat.		
Acc.		
Abl.		

Second Declension Masc. Noun

	Singular	Plural
Nom.	puer	
Gen.		
Dat.		
Acc.		
Abl.		

Translation: Translate each sentence into Latin.

EXAMPLE: The camel walks.		The camels walk.	
__camel-us__	__ambula-t__	__camel-i__	__ambula-nt__
Nom/Sg/Masc.	Verb Stem + 3rd/Sg	Nom/Pl/Masc.	Verb Stem + 3rd/Pl

1. The queen sings.

   _____   _____
   Nom/Sg/Fem   Verb Stem + 3rd/Sg

2. The queens sing.

   _____   _____
   Nom/**Pl**/Fem   Verb Stem + 3rd/**Pl**

3. The boy is a friend.

   _____   _____   _____
   Nom/Sg/Masc   LV 3rd/Sg   Nom/Sg/Masc

4. The boys are friends.

   _____   _____   _____
   Nom/**Pl**/Masc   LV 3rd/**Pl**   Nom/**Pl**/Masc

5. The temple is a building.

   _____   _____   _____
   Nom/Sg/Neut   LV 3rd/Sg   Nom/Sg/Neut

6. The temples are buildings.

   _____   _____   _____
   Nom/**Pl**/Neut   LV 3rd/**Pl**   Nom/**Pl**/Neut

Translation: Translate these sentences into English.

1. Viri sunt aquarii, et feminae sunt reginae.

2. Puer laborat, et puella in silvā ambulat.

3. Templum et castellum sunt aedificia.

4. Donum est frumentum et vinum.

5. Sumus discipuli, sed estis elephanti.

6. Christus est Deus, et Christus est vir.

WEEK 12: First and Second Declension Adjectives

Goals: Decline a first and second declension adjective and modify a singular noun with it.

Vocabulary

clámo, clamáre, clamávi, clamátum CLAH-moh, clah-MAH-ray, clah-MAH-vee, clah-MAH-toom	I shout, to shout, I shouted, shouted
bónus, bóna, bónum BOH-noose, BOH-nah, BOH-noom	good
fóedus, fóeda, fóedum FAY-doose, FAY-dah, FAY-doom	ugly
irátus, iráta, irátum ee-RAH-toose, ee-RAH-tah, ee-RAH-toom	angry
láetus, láeta, láetum LAY-toose, LAY-tah, LAY-toom	happy
málus, mála, málum MAH-loose, MAH-lah, MAH-loom	bad, evil
mágnus, mágna, mágnum MONG-noose, MONG-nah, MONG-noom	great, large
míser, mísera, míserum MEE-sair, MEE-sair-ah, MEE-sair-oom	sad, wretched
párvus, párva, párvum PAR-voose, PAR-vah, PAR-voom	small, little
púlcher, púlchra, púlchrum PUL-cur, PUL-crah, PUL-croom	beautiful, handsome
stúltus, stúlta, stúltum STUL-toose, STUL-tah, STUL-toom	foolish

Chant: First and Second Declension Noun/Adjective Endings

	Masculine Singular	Feminine Singular	Neuter Singular	Masculine Plural	Feminine Plural	Neuter Plural
Nominative	-us/-r	-a	-um	-i	-ae	-a
Genitive	-i	-ae	-i	-orum	-arum	-orum
Dative	-o	-ae	-o	-is	-is	-is
Accusative	-um	-am	-um	-os	-as	-a
Ablative	-o	a	-o	-is	-is	-is

Grammar Lesson

An **adjective** is a word that modifies a noun. Adjectives answer the questions: which one? what kind? or how many? In Latin, adjectives must match the noun they go with in **case, number, and gender**. That means if the noun is Nominative case, the adjective must be Nominative too. If the noun is plural, then the adjective must be plural. If the noun is Masculine, then the adjective must be Masculine.

First and Second Declension Adjectives have endings just like the nouns we have learned. Nouns can only be one gender, but adjectives can be all three genders!

In English, adjectives come before the noun they modify, but in Latin, the adjective usually comes **after** the noun.

Grammar Sound Off

A noun is a person…	…a place, a thing, an idea!
An adjective is a word…	…that modifies a noun.
An adjective matches its noun…	…in case, number, and gender.
A noun has only *one* gender…	…an adjective has all *three*!

MYTHOLOGY

Minerva was the Roman goddess of wisdom, crafts, and later on war. Her Greek name was **Athena**. After the Trojan war, she helped the hero Odysseus get back to his home. The story is told in the *Odyssey*.

WEEK 12: Worksheet   Nomen: _____

Vocabulary: Fill in the missing parts in English and in Latin.

clamo			
			shouted

| bonus | bona | bonum | |

| foedus | | | |

| | | | angry |

| | laeta | | |

| | | | bad, evil |

| | | magnum | |

| miser | | | |

| parvus | | | |

| | pulchra | | |

| | | | foolish |

Paideia Latina, Level A | 73

Chants: Complete the chants by filling in the empty boxes.

	Singular	English	Plural	English
1st Person				
2nd Person				
3rd Person			clama-nt	they shout

	Singular	English	Plural	English
1st Person				
2nd Person				
3rd Person	est	he/she/it is		

Chant: First and Second Declension Adjective

	Masculine Singular	Feminine Singular	Neuter Singular	Masculine Plural	Feminine Plural	Neuter Plural
Nom	bonus	bona	bonum			
Gen						
Dat						
Acc						
Abl				bonis	bonis	bonis

Second Declension Masculine Noun/Adjective Pair

	Singular	Plural
Nominative	camelus malus	

Grammar: Fill in the blanks with info from your grammar and grammar sound-off from this week or from previous weeks.

1. A _____ is a person, place, thing, or idea.
2. An _____ is a word that modifies a noun.
3. An adjective must match a noun in case, number, and _____.
4. Nouns can only be _____ gender, but adjectives can be all _____ genders.

Picturae: Draw a quick picture of each of these things.

bonus vir	foedus puer	irata ursa
laeta puella	malus lupus	magnus camelus
misera magistra / stultus discipulus	parvus elephantus	pulchra femina

Adjectives: Circle the correct form of each adjective to go with the noun, then translate both the noun and the adjective.

elephantus (**magnus** / magna / magnum) = large elephant

1. camelus (iratus / irata / iratum) = _____

2. oppidum (parvus / parva / parvum) = _____

3. regina (pulcher / pulchra / pulchrum) = _____

4. lupus (foedus / foeda / foedum) = _____

5. donum (bonus / bona / bonum) = _____

6. puella (stultus / stulta / stultum) = _____

Fabula: Read the story below, trying to understand the Latin words mixed in with the English words. (You do not have to write anything down.)

Laeta Puella

Once there was a **pulchra puella** who **laborat** for her **mala** stepmother **et foedae** step-sisters. Whenever the **foedae** step-sisters want something, **clamant**, "Cinderella!" **Et pulchra puella** goes to do whatever **rogant**. One day the **pulcher** prince held a **magnus** ball. **Misera puella** wants to go, **sed** she only has a **foedus** dress. Her **bona** fairy godmother appears and makes her a **pulcher** dress and makes a carriage out of a **parvus** pumpkin. The last **donum** the **bona** godmother **dat** her **est** a pair of glass slippers. **Laeta puella** goes to the **magnus** ball and dances with the **pulcher** prince. **Stultae** step-sisters think the prince **amat** them, **sed** the prince **amat pulchra puella**. She runs away at midnight, **et** leaves behind a **parvus** glass slipper. The **pulcher** prince searches the **magnum oppidum** for her until he find her. He tries the glass slipper on her **parvus** foot. It fits! Now the **laeta puella** does not have to live with her **mala** stepmother **et iratae** step-sisters. She will live in the **castellum** with the **pulcher** prince and one day the **pulchra puella** will be **regina**.

WEEK 13: First and Second Declension Adjectives; Predicate Adjectives

*Goals: Modify a plural noun with an adjective
and use predicate adjectives in sentences.*

Vocabulary

vóco, vocáre, vocávi, vocátum VOH-coh, voh-CAH-ray, voh-CAH-vee, voh-CAH-toom	I call, to call, I called, called
antíquus, antíqua, antíquum an-TEE-kwoose, an-TEE-kwah, an-TEE-kwoom	old
áptus, ápta, áptum AHP-toose, AHP-tah, AHP-toom	fitting, suitable
cárus, cára, cárum CAH-roose, CAH-rah, CAH-room	dear
dúbius, dúbia, dúbium DOO-bee-oose, DOO-bee-ah, DOO-bee-oom	doubtful
fálsus, fálsa, fálsum FALL-soose, FALL-sah, FALL-soom	false
méus, méa, méum MAY-oose, MAY-ah, MAY-oom	my, mine
nóvus, nóva, nóvum NOH-voose, NOH-vah, NOH-voom	new
parátus, paráta, parátum pah-RAH-toose, pah-RAH-tah, pah-RAH-toom	prepared
túus, túa, túum TOO-oose, TOO-ah, TOO-oom	your, yours
vérus, véra, vérum VAY-roose, VAY-rah, VAY-room	true

Chant: First and Second Declension Adjective Endings

	Masculine Singular	Feminine Singular	Neuter Singular	Masculine Plural	Feminine Plural	Neuter Plural
Nominative	-us/-r	-a	-um	-i	-ae	-a
Genitive	-i	-ae	-i	-orum	-arum	-orum
Dative	-o	-ae	-o	-is	-is	-is
Accusative	-um	-am	-um	-os	-as	-a
Ablative	-o	a	-o	-is	-is	-is

Grammar Lesson

Since adjectives have to modify the nouns they go with in case, number, and gender, when the noun becomes plural, the adjective must become plural too.

femina pulchra	→	feminae pulchrae	=	beautiful women
puer bonus	→	pueri boni	=	good boys
aedificium foedum	→	aedificia foeda	=	ugly buildings

If we connect a noun to an adjective with a linking verb, then we call that adjective a **predicate adjective**.

Elephantus est magnus.	=	The elephant is large.
Discipula est stulta.	=	The female student is foolish.
Aquarii sunt laeti.	=	The water-carriers are happy.

The predicate adjective must still match its noun in case, number, and gender.

Grammar Sound Off

Review sound off from last week and previous weeks.

 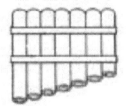 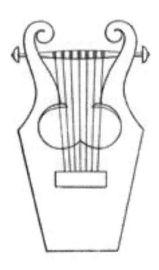

WEEK 13: Worksheet   Nomen: _____

Vocabulary: Fill in the missing parts in English and in Latin.

voco			
	to call		

| antiquus | antiqua | antiquum | |

| aptus | | | |

| | | | dear |

| | | dubium | |

| | falsa | | |

| | | | my, mine |

| novus | | | |

| paratus | | | |

| | | tuum | |

| | | | true |

Paideia Latina, Level A | 79

Second Declension Masculine Noun/Adjective Pair

	Singular	Plural
Nominative	vir antiquus	

Second Declension Feminine Noun/Adjective Pair

	Singular	Plural
Nominative	rosa tua	

Second Declension Neuter Noun/Adjective Pair

	Singular	Plural
Nominative	forum novum	

True/False/Doubtful: Read through each Latin sentence and mark it as true, false, or doubtful (if you're not sure), using the Latin words.

	Verus	Falsus	Dubius

    Magister est vir.   Verus

1. Camelus est elephantus. _____
2. Casa est aedificium. _____
3. Puellae sunt aquarii. _____
4. Cibus est bonus. _____
5. Regina est femina. _____
6. Puer est antiquus. _____
7. Femina est vir. _____
8. Elephantus est magnus. _____

Matching: Draw straight lines matching each noun to the adjective that could go with it. (Look at endings!) Some may have more than one option.

Noun	Adjective
Germanae	Parva
Filius	Novum
Frumentum	Laetae
Sella	Magni
Fluvii	Antiqua
Oppida	Meus

(Germanae is matched to Laetae)

Picturae: Draw pictures of the following <u>plural</u> noun/adjective pairs.

pulchrae rosae	antiqua castella (neut. pl.!)	amici cari

Plurals: Make the sentence plural by changing <u>each</u> word. Then, translate.

EXAMPLE: Lupus est foedus. → *Lupi sunt foedi.* = The wolves are ugly.

1. Casa est parva. → _____

   = _____

2. Vinum est aptum. → _____

   = _____

3. Donum est novum. → _____

   = _____

4. Equus est meus. → _____

   = _____

5. Cena est bona. → _____

   = _____

6. Hortus est tuus. → _____

   = _____

EXAMPLE: *Femina misera orat.* → *Feminae miserae orant.* = The sad women pray.

7. Puella pulchra ambulat. → _____

   = _____

8. Magister paratus vocat. → _____

   = _____

9. Aedificium antiquum stat. → _____

   = _____

Derivatives: Use your knowledge of Latin vocabulary to fill in the blanks.

1. The word "apt" comes from *aptus*. An apt answer is one that is _____ for the question.

2. The word "antiquity" comes from *antiquus*. The study of antiquity is the study of the _____ days before Christ.

3. The word "dubious" comes from *dubius*. If someone makes a dubious claim, then their claim is _____.

4. The word "innovate" comes from *novus*. An innovation is a _____ idea or product.

5. The word "verify" comes from *verus*. If you verify a statement, you check to see if it is _____.

Fabula: Read the story below, trying to understand the Latin words mixed in with the English words. (You do not have to write anything down.)

Malus Dragon

This **est fabula** that may **non** be **aptus** for **parvi pueri et parvae puellae**. If **mea fabula** frightens you, cover **tuae** ears. **Est fabula** of **malus, foedus, antiquus** dragon who lives in a cave **in silvā**. The **malus** dragon **amat** to eat **parvi pueri et parvae puellae**. One day, **stultus puer et** his **carus amicus errant in silvā. Sunt** lost, **et vocant** for help, **sed** the only one who hears **stulti pueri est malus** dragon. **Foedus** dragon finds some branches **et flat** on them to make a **novus** fire at the mouth of the cave. The **miseri pueri** see the smoke **et** come running through the **silva**. "**Est casa** nearby?" **dubii pueri rogant** each other. "**Est castellum?**" **Non, est** only a campfire. **Malus** dragon hides in the shadows of the cave. He speaks **falsa** words and pretends to be **antiqua femina**. "Come inside, **mei cari pueri!** I have **tua cena parata!**" The words **non sunt vera**, but **stulti pueri non** stop to consider. **Intrant** the cave, **et sunt** never seen again.

WEEK 14: Noun Jobs

Goals: List the noun jobs that each case does and label them in simple English sentences.

Vocabulary

aedífico, aedificáre, aedificávi, aedificátum ay-DEE-fee-coh, ay-dee-fee-CAH-ray, ay-dee-fee-CAH-vee, ay-dee-fee-CAH-toom	I build, to build, I built, built
ástrum, ástri (n.) AH-stroom, AH-stree	star
cubículum, cubículi (n.) coo-BEE-coo-loom, coo-BEE-coo-lee	bedroom
culína, culínae (f.) coo-LEE-nah, coo-LEE-nay	kitchen
fénestra, fénestrae (f.) FEN-eh-strah, FEN-eh-stray	window
iánua, iánuae (f.) YAWN-oo-ah, YAWN-oo-ay	door
lúna, lúnae (f.) LOO-nah, LOO-nay	moon
múrus, múri (m.) MOO-roose, MOO-ree	wall
pórta, pórtae (f.) POR-tah, POR-tay	gate
stélla, stéllae (f.) STEL-lah, STEL-lay	star
téctum, técti (n.) TEC-toom, TEC-tee	roof

Highlight Masculine nouns with blue, Feminine with pink, and Neuter with yellow.

84 | Paideia Latina, Level A

Chant: Cases, Jobs, and Translations

CASE	JOB	Singular	Plural
Nominative	SN, PRN	the *noun*	the *nouns*
Genitive	PNA	of the *noun*, the *noun's*	of the *nouns*, the *nouns'*
Dative	IO	to/for the *noun*	to/for the *nouns*
Accusative	DO, OP	the *noun*	the *nouns*
Ablative	OP	by/with/from the *noun*	by/with/from the *nouns*

Grammar Lesson

In English we use **word order** to show what "job" a noun is doing in the sentence. The subject noun comes before the verb. The direct object comes after the verb.

> The **man** eats the **chicken**.
>
> ...means something very different than....
>
> The **chicken** eats the **man**.

In Latin, it doesn't matter what order the words are in because the **ending** of the noun tells us what job the noun is doing in the sentence. You already know that the Nominative endings are used for subject nouns and predicate Nominatives. This week we are going to memorize which noun jobs each of the other cases do, and we are going to memorize how to translate each case into English.

> Nominative: Subject Noun (SN), Predicate Nominative (PRN)
>
> Genitive: Possessive Noun Adjective (PNA)
>
> Dative: Indirect Object (IO)
>
> Accusative: Direct Object (DO), Object of the Preposition (OP)
>
> Ablative: Object of the Preposition (OP)

On our worksheet, we will practice labeling subject nouns (SN), predicate Nominatives (PRN), and direct objects (DO). You will be able to find the subject nouns easily. To tell the difference between a PRN and a DO, remember that:

> A Predicate Nominative **renames the subject.**
>
> A Direct Object **receives the action** from the verb.

Grammar Sound Off

What are the noun jobs, noun jobs, noun jobs,

What are the noun jobs for each case?

Nominative Case!

Subject Noun, SN. Predicate Nominative, PRN.

Genitive Case!

Possessive Noun Adjective, PNA.

Dative Case!

Indirect Object, IO.

Accusative Case!

Direct Object, DO. Object of the Preposition, OP.

Ablative Case!

Object of the Preposition, OP.

These are the noun jobs, noun jobs, noun jobs,

These are the noun jobs for each case.

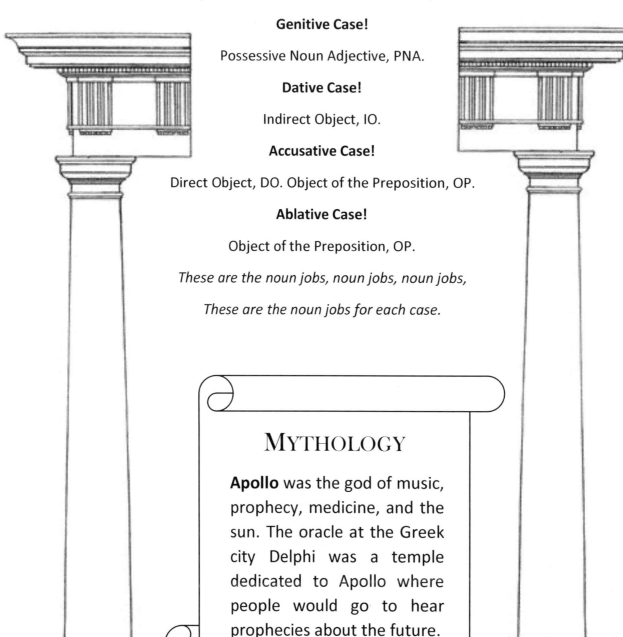

Mythology

Apollo was the god of music, prophecy, medicine, and the sun. The oracle at the Greek city Delphi was a temple dedicated to Apollo where people would go to hear prophecies about the future.

WEEK 14: Worksheet   Nomen: _____

Vocabulary: Fill in the missing parts in English and in Latin.

aedifico			
I build			

| astrum | astri | n. | |

| cubiculum | | | |

| | | | kitchen |

| | fenestrae | | |

| | ianuae | | |

| | | | moon |

| murus | | | |

| porta | | | |

| stella | | | |

| | | | roof |

Paideia Latina, Level A | 87

Matching: Draw a straight line matching the case to the correct noun job. Some cases will need two jobs!

Nominative   Possessive Noun Adjective

                                              Subject Noun
Genitive
                                              Indirect Object

Dative   Predicate Nominative

                                              Object of the Preposition
Accusative
                                              Object of the Preposition

Ablative   Direct Object

Chants: Fill in the missing blanks on the chant.

CASE	JOB	Singular	Plural
Dative			to/for the *nouns*
	OP	by/with/from the *noun*	

Abbreviations: Write out the full meaning for each abbreviation.

SN: _____

PRN: _____

PNA: _____

IO: _____

DO: _____

OP: _____

Picturae: Draw a picture with all of these things in it and label the things with the Latin word.

astrum	cubiculum	culina	fenestra	ianua
luna	murus	porta	stella	tectum

Labeling: Label each noun in the sentence with the following jobs and cases: SN-Nom, PRN-Nom, DO-Acc.

>   SN-NOM   PRN-NOM
> The woman is a teacher.   (Predicate Nominative **renames the subject**!)
>
>   SN-NOM   DO-ACC
> The brother builds a house.   (Direct Object **receives the action** from the verb!)

1. The girl is a friend.
2. The man tells a story.
3. The field is a garden.
4. The students are boys.
5. The water-carrier carries water.
6. The door is a gate.
7. The road enters the forest.
8. The teachers call the students.
9. The rivers are water.
10. My sister gives a gift.

Fabula: Read the story below. (You do not have to write anything down.)

> **Nova Casa**
>
> I need a **nova casa** because **mea casa est** too **parva**. **Meum cubiculum** can only hold **mensa et sella**, not a bed! **Mea culina** can only hold enough **cibus** for one **cena**! **Mea porta est** too **parva** for **elephantus ambulare** through. **Mea ianua est** too **parva** for **ursa intrare**. **Meum tectum est** too low for the head of **camelus**. **Mea fenestra est** too **parva** to see **luna et stellae**! I have to go outside **mea casa** to see **astra**. **Mea casa non est apta** for me. I ought to tear down **muri** of **mea casa et aedificare nova, magna casa**.

WEEK 15: Noun Jobs Continued; PAINS

Goals: Label noun jobs in more complex English sentences, and identify and use masculine first declension exceptions.

Vocabulary

	iúvo, iuváre, iúvi, iútum YOO-voh, yoo-VAH-ray, YOO-vee, YOO-toom	I help, to help, I helped, helped
	poéta, poétae (m.) poh-AY-tah, poh-AY-tay	poet
	piráta, pirátae (m.) pee-RAH-tah, pee-RAH-tay	pirate
	agrícola, agrícolae (m.) ah-GREE-coh-lah, ah-GREE-coh-lay	farmer
	auríga, aurígae (m.) ow-REE-gah, ow-REE-jay	charioteer
	íncola, íncolae (m.) EEN-coh-lah, EEN-coh-lay	settler
	náuta, náutae (m.) NOW-tah, NOW-tay	sailor
	scríba, scríbae (m.) SCREE-bah, SCREE-bay	scribe
	táberna, tábernae (f.) TAH-ber-nah, TAH-ber-nay	a shop
	tabernárius, tabernárii (m.) tah-ber-NAH-ree-oose, tah-ber-NAH-ree-ee	shopkeeper
	túmulus, túmuli (m.) TOOM-yoo-loose, TOOM-yoo-lee	hill

Highlight Masculine nouns with blue, Feminine with pink, and Neuter with yellow.

Chant: Cases, Jobs, and Translation of a Given Noun

CASE	JOB	Singular	Plural
Nominative	SN, PRN	the *horse*	the *horses*
Genitive	PNA	of the *horse*, the *horse's*	of the *horses*, the *horses'*
Dative	IO	to/for the *horse*	to/for the *horses*
Accusative	DO, OP	the *horse*	the *horses*
Ablative	OP	by/with/from the *horse*	by/with/from the *horses*

First Declension Masculine EXCEPTION Noun/Adjective Pair

	Singular	Plural
Nominative	agricola bonus	agricolae boni
Genitive	agricolae boni	agricolarum bonorum
Dative	agricolae bono	agricolis bonis
Accusative	agricolam bonum	agricolas bonos
Ablative	agricolā bono	agricolis bonis

Grammar Lesson

This week we will practice labeling noun jobs in English sentences. On our worksheet, we will practice labeling subject nouns (SN), predicate Nominatives (PRN), and direct objects (DO), possessive noun adjectives (PNA), and objects of the preposition (OP).

A Subject Noun **does the verb.**

A Predicate Nominative **renames the subject.**

A Direct Object **receives the action** from the verb.

A Possessive Noun Adjective **shows ownership** with an apostrophe or "of"

An Object of the Preposition **follows a preposition** (such as "in" or "with")

We also have some **first declension masculine exceptions** in our wordlist. These words look feminine and use feminine endings, but they are really masculine! That means that if you put an adjective with them, then the adjective must use masculine endings.

agric**a** bon**us** = the good farmer

naut**a** mal**us** = the bad sailor

These exceptions are "pains" to remember, but we can remember them by using the acronym "PAINS."

P = poeta (poet); pirata (pirate)

A = agricola (farmer); auriga (charioteer)

I = incola (settler)

N = nauta (sailor)

S = scriba (scribe)

You will notice that all the masculine exceptions are professions (jobs) that only men would have had in the ancient world.

Grammar Sound Off

Review the noun jobs chant from last week.

MYTHOLOGY

Diana was the twin sister of Apollo. Her Greek name was **Artemis**. Diana was a huntress who lived in the forest and refused to marry. She was also the goddess of the moon. There was a great temple to Diana in the city of Ephesus in what is now Turkey. The Apostle Paul visited Ephesus on a missionary journey and encountered worshipers of Diana.

WEEK 15: Worksheet   Nomen: _____

Vocabulary: Fill in the missing parts in English and in Latin.

iuvo			
	to help		

| poeta | poetae | m. | |

| pirata | | | |

| | agricolae | | |

| | | | charioteer |

| | incolae | | |

| | | | sailor |

| | | | scribe |

| taberna | | | |

| | tabernarii | | |

| | | | hill |

94 | Paideia Latina, Level A

Chant: Fill in this chant using the English word "girl."

CASE	JOB	Singular	Plural
	SN, PRN	the girl	
			to/for the girls
Accusative			

First Declension Masculine EXCEPTIONS Noun/Adjective Pair

	Singular	Plural
Nominative	pirata malus	
Genitive		
Dative		
Accusative		
Ablative		

	Singular	Plural
Nominative	scriba dubius	
Genitive		
Dative		
Accusative		
Ablative		

Write down all the first declension masculine exception "PAINS":

P_____   P_____   A_____

A_____   I_____   N_____

S_____

Abbreviations: Write out the full meaning for each abbreviation.

SN: _____

PRN: _____

PNA: _____

IO: _____

DO: _____

OP: _____

Labeling: Label each noun in the sentence with the following jobs and cases: SN-Nom, PRN-Nom, DO-Acc, PNA-Gen, OP-Abl (Use PNA-Gen for 's or "of"!)

>   PNA-GEN   SN-NOM   PRN-NOM   OP-ABL
> The woman's daughter is a teacher in the school.
>
>   SN-NOM   PNA-GEN   DO-ACC   OP-ABL
> The brother of the shopkeeper builds a shop with his sister.

1. The girl is a friend of the queen in the castle.   (of the queen = the queen's)

2. The man with the teacher's pen tells a story.

3. The farmer's field is a garden of roses.   (of roses = roses')

4. The students with the chairs are the teacher's sons.

5. The camel and the elephant carry the water of the town.   (of the town = town's)

Translation: Translate these noun/adjective pairs into Latin in the nominative case. Watch out for singulars and plurals. Remember that the PAINS *look* feminine but their adjectives are masculine!

prepared farmer	→	agricola paratus
handsome poets	→	poetae pulchri

1. large charioteer → _____
2. large charioteers → _____
3. good sailor → _____
4. good sailors → _____
5. old scribe → _____
6. happy pirates → _____
7. suitable settler → _____
8. new farmers → _____

Fabula: Read the story below. (You do not have to write anything down.)

Auriga et Poeta

Auriga et poeta sunt germani who live **in casā** on **tumulus. Auriga est magnus, sed poeta est parvus. Auriga est foedus, sed poeta est pulcher. Auriga laborat in campus** outside **oppidum** with his **equi. Poeta ambulat in forum in oppidum. Narrat** his poems to **tabernarii in tabernae.** Narrat his poems to **nautae laeti, et incolae stulti, et scribae antiqui. Sed** no one **amat** the poems of **poeta pulcher.** One **agricola dubius dat** a coin to the **poeta, sed** he does not want to listen to **poeta paratus. Agricola dubius** wants **poeta miser** to go away! At the end of the day, **auriga magnus et poeta parvus intrant** the **porta** of their **casa** on **tumulus. Auriga magnus** has **multae rosae et** coins from **viri et feminae** who watched him race, **sed poeta parvus** has only one **parvus** coin.

WEEK 16: REVIEW

Goals: Retain and recall vocabulary and grammar from weeks 12-15.

Vocabulary
Check off the ones you know.

☐	**aedifico**	I build	☐	**malus**	bad, evil
☐	**agricola**	farmer	☐	**meus**	my, mine
☐	**antiquus**	old	☐	**miser**	sad, wretched
☐	**aptus**	fitting, suitable	☐	**murus**	wall
☐	**astrum**	star	☐	**nauta**	sailor
☐	**auriga**	charioteer	☐	**novus**	new
☐	**bonus**	good	☐	**paratus**	prepared
☐	**carus**	dear	☐	**parvus**	small, little
☐	**clamo**	I shout	☐	**pirata**	pirate
☐	**cubiculum**	bedroom	☐	**poeta**	poet
☐	**culina**	kitchen	☐	**porta**	gate
☐	**dubius**	doubtful	☐	**pulcher**	beautiful, handsome
☐	**falsus**	false	☐	**scriba**	scribe
☐	**fenestra**	window	☐	**stella**	star
☐	**foedus**	ugly	☐	**stultus**	foolish
☐	**ianua**	door	☐	**taberna**	shop
☐	**incola**	settler	☐	**tabernarius**	shopkeeper
☐	**iratus**	angry	☐	**tectum**	roof
☐	**iuvo**	I help	☐	**tumulus**	hill
☐	**laetus**	happy	☐	**tuus**	your
☐	**luna**	moon	☐	**verus**	true
☐	**magnus**	large, great	☐	**voco**	I call

WEEK 16: Review Worksheet   Nomen: _____

Derivatives: Give an English derivative for each Latin root.

1. Root: miser   Derivative: miserable, misery
2. Root: agricola   Derivative: _____
3. Root: ianua   Derivative: _____
4. Root: luna   Derivative: _____
5. Root: astrum   Derivative: _____
6. Root: porta   Derivative: _____
7. Root: antiquus   Derivative: _____
8. Root: clamo   Derivative: _____

Write down all the first declension masculine exception "PAINS":

P_____   P_____   A_____

A_____   I_____   N_____

S_____

Grammar: Label each noun in the sentence with the following jobs and cases: SN-Nom, PRN-Nom, DO-Acc, PNA-Gen, and OP-Abl

1. The wretched <u>camel</u> carries the <u>settler's</u> <u>water</u> on the <u>road</u>.

2. The <u>sister</u> of the <u>boy</u> in the <u>marketplace</u> is a <u>teacher</u>.   (of the boy = the boy's)

3. The <u>queen's</u> <u>brother</u> helps the <u>farmer's</u> <u>horse</u>.

Paideia Latina, Level A | 99

Vocabulary: Fill in the crossword puzzle with vocabulary from chapters 12-15.

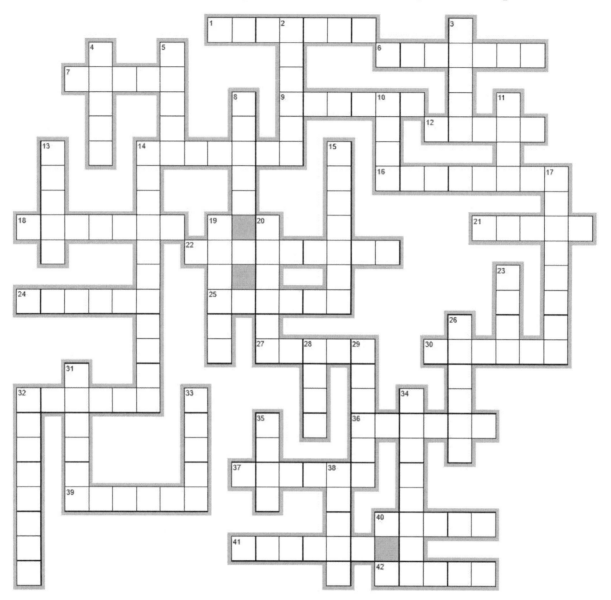

Word Bank

AEDIFICO AGRICOLA ANTIQUUS APTUS ASTRUM AURIGA BONUS CARUS CLAMO
CUBICULUM CULINA DUBIUS FALSUS FENESTRA FOEDUS IANUA INCOLA IRATUS
IUVO LAETUS LUNA MAGNUS MALUS MEUS MISER MURUS NAUTA NOVUS
PARATUS PARVUS PIRATA POETA PORTA PULCHER SCRIBA STELLA STULTUS
TABERNA TABERNARIUS TECTUM TUMULUS TUUS VERUS VOCO

Across

1. prepared
6. foolish
7. sailor
9. settler
12. new
14. shop
16. farmer
18. beautiful, handsome
21. gate
22. bedroom
24. kitchen
25. angry
27. fitting, suitable
30. false
32. ugly
36. happy
37. scribe
39. large, great
40. sad, wretched
41. star
42. poet

Down

2. charioteer
3. I shout
4. bad, evil
5. door
8. wall
10. moon
11. I help
13. true
14. shopkeeper
15. hill
17. old
19. doubtful
20. pirate
23. my, mine
26. small, little
28. your, yours
29. star
31. roof
32. window
33. dear
34. I build
35. I call
38. good

Chants: Complete the chants by filling in the empty boxes.

	Singular	English	Plural	English
1st Person	iuvo	I help		
2nd Person				
3rd Person				

	Singular	English	Plural	English
1st Person				
2nd Person				
3rd Person			sunt	they are

Chant: First and Second Declension Adjective

	Masculine Singular	Feminine Singular	Neuter Singular	Masculine Plural	Feminine Plural	Neuter Plural
Nom	miser	misera	miserum			
Gen						
Dat						
Acc						
Abl				miseris	miseris	miseris

Second Declension Neuter Noun/Adjective Pair

	Singular	Plural
Nominative	donum aptum	
Genitive		
Dative		
Accusative		
Ablative		

First Declension Masculine EXCEPTIONS Noun/Adjective Pair

	Singular	Plural
Nominative	nauta iratus	
Genitive		
Dative		
Accusative		
Ablative		

Noun Cases, Jobs, and Translations

CASE	JOB	Singular	Plural
		the *house*	
Genitive			
			to/for the *houses*
	OP		

Translation: Translate each sentence into English.

1. Auriga magnus et poeta parvus sunt germani.

2. Femina pulchra est magistra bona.

3. Discipuli stulti clamant, sed discipulae bonae iuvant.

4. Tabernarius laetus in tabernā laborat, sed femina cara in culinā laborat.

5. Luna non est stella, et fenestra non est ianua.

Translation: Translate each sentence into Latin.

EXAMPLE: The happy sailor shouts.		
__naut-a__	__laet-us__	__clama-t__
Nom/Sg/Masc.	Nom/Sg/Masc.	Verb Stem + 3rd/Sg

1. The true farmer helps.

   _____   _____   _____
   Nom/Sg/Masc*   Nom/Sg/Masc   Verb Stem + 3rd/Sg

2. The true farmers help.

   _____   _____   _____
   Nom/**Pl**/Masc*   Nom/**Pl**/Masc   Verb Stem + 3rd/**Pl**

3. The girl is beautiful.

   _____   _____   _____
   Nom/Sg/Fem   LV 3rd/Sg   Nom/Sg/Fem

4. The old scribes are men.

   _____   _____   _____   _____
   Nom/**Pl**/Masc*   Nom/**Pl**/Masc   LV 3rd/**Pl**   Nom/**Pl**/Masc

* Masculine exceptions! Remember that the PAINS look feminine but are really masculine!

WEEK 17: Accusative Case: Direct Object

*Goals: Put nouns in the Accusative case
and translate singular direct objects in Latin sentences.*

Vocabulary

óccupo, occupáre, occupávi, occupátum OH-coo-poh, oh-coo-PAH-ray, oh-coo-PAH-vee, oh-coo-PAH-toom	I seize, to seize, I seized, seized
gálea, gáleae (f.) GAH-lay-ah, GAH-lay-ay	helmet
gládius, gládii (m.) GLAH-dee-oose, GLAH-dee-ee	sword
haréna, harénae (f.) ha-RAY-nah, ha-RAY-nay	sand
hásta, hástae (f.) HA-stah, HA-stay	spear
línea, líneae (f.) LEE-nay-ah, LEE-nay-ay	line, string
ságitta, ságittae (f.) SAH-jee-tah, SAH-jee-tay	arrow
sagittárius, sagittárii (m.) sah-jee-TAW-ree-oose, sah-jee-TAW-ree-ee	archer
scútum, scúti (n.) SCOO-toom, SCOO-tee	shield
síca, sícae (f.) SEE-cah, SEE-chay	dagger
victória, victóriae (f.) vic-TOH-ree-ah, vic-TOH-ree-ay	victory

Highlight Masculine nouns with blue, Feminine with pink, and Neuter with yellow.

Chant: First and Second Declension Noun/Adjective Endings

	Masculine Singular	Feminine Singular	Neuter Singular	Masculine Plural	Feminine Plural	Neuter Plural
Nominative	-us/-r	-a	-um	-i	-ae	-a
Genitive	-i	-ae	-i	-orum	-arum	-orum
Dative	-o	-ae	-o	-is	-is	-is
Accusative	**-um**	**-am**	**-um**	**-os**	**-as**	**-a**
Ablative	-o	a	-o	-is	-is	-is

Grammar Lesson

This week our translation sentences are getting a lot more fun! We are learning how to use the direct object in Latin. A **direct object** receives the action of the verb. If you remember from our noun jobs chant, the **Accusative case** is for the direct object. This means that anytime we want to use a direct object in a Latin sentence, we have to put an Accusative ending on it. The chant above has all the Accusative endings highlighted, and here they are written out below:

　　First Declension Fem.　　　-am (sg.)　　-as (pl.)

　　Second Declension Masc.　　-um (sg.)　　-os (pl.)

　　Second Declension Masc.　　-um (sg.)　　-a (pl.)

In Latin, the direct object typically comes after the subject and before the verb. The sentence pattern usually looks like this: **SN – DO – V**. But (warning!) sometimes the words will be in a different order.

Here are some sentences that use direct objects. Look at the endings!

　　Puella equ**um** amat.　=　The girl loves the horse.

　　Equus puell**am** amat.　=　The horse loves the girl.

　　Regina don**um** dat.　=　The queen gives a gift.

Notice in the last sentence that the neuter word "donum" could be either Nominative or Accusative, since the **neuter rule** states that both those cases will match each other. When we translate, we have to figure out if the word is acting as a subject or a direct object. Since "Regina" has to be Nominative, we already have a subject, so by process of elimination, we conclude that "donum" is actually Accusative. It is acting as a direct object.

Grammar Sound Off

The Direct Object receives...	...the action of the verb.
To make a Direct Object...	...use the Accusative.
-am, -am, -am in the Singular Feminine...	...-as, -as, -as in the Plural Feminine.
-um, -um, -um in the Singular Masculine...	...-os, -os, -os in the Plural Masculine.
-um, -um, -um in the Singular Neuter...	...-a, -a, -a in the Plural Neuter.
The neuter rule states...	...the Nominative matches the Accusative,
And in the plural those cases...	...always have an A.
Subjects and direct objects...	...look the same in the Neuter.
When translating use the case...	...that makes the most sense.

WEEK 17: Worksheet   Nomen: _____

Vocabulary: Fill in the missing parts in English and in Latin.

occupo			
		I seized	

| galea | galeae | f. | |

| gladius | | | |

| | harenae | | |

| | | | spear |

| | | | line, string |

| | sagittae | | |

| | sagittarii | | |

| scutum | | | |

| | sicae | | |

| | | | victory |

108 | Paideia Latina, Level A

Grammar: Fill in the blanks with info from your grammar and grammar sound-off from this week or from previous weeks.

1. A _____ _____ receives action from the verb.
2. We use the _____ case for the direct object.
3. In the _____ gender, the nominative and accusative cases look the same.
4. When translating a neuter word, we use the case that makes the most _____.

Chants: Complete the chants by filling in the empty boxes.

	Singular	English	Plural	English
1st Person				
2nd Person	occupas	you seize		
3rd Person				

	Singular	English	Plural	English
1st Person				
2nd Person			estis	you all are
3rd Person				

First and Second Declension Endings: Fill in the Accusative

	Masculine Singular	Feminine Singular	Neuter Singular	Masculine Plural	Feminine Plural	Neuter Plural
Nominative	-us/-r	-a	-um	-i	-ae	-a
Genitive	-i	-ae	-i	-orum	-arum	-orum
Dative	-o	-ae	-o	-is	-is	-is
Ablative	-o	a	-o	-is	-is	-is

Word Hunt: Choose the best word from the box to put in each of the sentences below.

| galea | gladius | harena | hasta | linea |
| sagitta | sagittarius | scutum | sica | victoria |

1. The _____ protects your head.
2. A _____ is a shorter version of a _____.
3. The _____ could not shoot the _____ because the _____ on his bow was broken.
4. The long, rectangular _____ protects the body of the soldier.
5. He threw the _____ with all his might and it landed thirty yards away on the _____.
6. The horse is prepared for the day of battle, but the _____ belongs to the Lord.

Matching: Draw a straight line matching the Gender/Number to the correct Nominative in the middle and the correct Accusative on the right.

GENDER/NUMBER	NOMINATIVE	ACCUSATIVE
Fem/Sg	-us	-um
Fem/Pl	-um	-um
Masc/Sg	-a	-as
Masc/Pl	-a	-am
Neut/Sg	-i	-os
Neut/Pl	-ae	-a

110 | Paideia Latina, Level A

Chant: Give the Accusative endings.

	Masculine Singular	Feminine Singular	Neuter Singular	Masculine Plural	Feminine Plural	Neuter Plural
Accusative						

Accusatives. Transform each singular nominative noun into the accusative case.

femina → femin**am**   puer → puer**um**

1. galea → _____
2. gladius → _____
3. scutum → _____
4. victoria → _____
5. hasta → _____
6. lupus → _____
7. hortus → _____
8. astrum → _____
9. sagittarius → _____
10. sica → _____

Translation: Translate these sentences from Latin to English.

Auriga hastam portat.   The charioteer carries a spear.

1. Vir scutum occupat.   _____
2. Femina sagittarium vocat. _____
3. Feminam sagittarius vocat. _____
4. Scutum vir occupat.   _____
5. Nauta sicam et gladium portat. _____
6. Sagittarius victoriam occupat. _____
7. Equum auriga amat.   _____
8. Agricola portam intrat.   _____
9. Serva fabulam narrat.   _____
10. Tabernarius oppidum intrat. _____

Labeling: Use Latin words to label the military items each arrow points to.

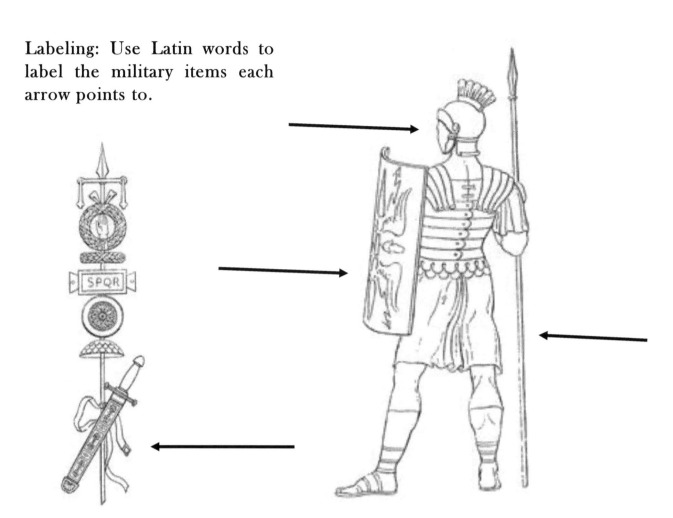

Fabula: Read the story below. (You do not have to write anything down.)

Sagittarius et Puella Parva

One day **malus dominus occupat puellam parvam** from the **forum** in **oppidum et** takes **puellam** to **castellum in silvā**. **Viri et feminae** in **oppidum sunt miseri. Rogant sagittarium** to save **puellam**. **Sagittarius parat** for the journey. **Sagittarius sagittas occupat. Sagittarius occupat scutum, et gladium, et sicam, et galeam. Sagittarius hastam non occupat**, because **hasta est** too **magna**. **Sagittarius paratus silvam intrat. Silva est magna, et sagittarius ambulat** for a long time. Finally, he sees **campum** in middle of **silva**. In the middle of the **campus est castellum** of **malus dominus. Porta est** open. **Sagittarius castellum intrat, sed** he trips over **linea** stretched across **harena. Est** trap! Five **mali viri** jump out and try **occupare sagittarium. Sagittarius** fights **malos viros** with his **sagittae et gladius** and has **victoriam**. Then **malus dominus** appears. **Dominus est magnus et foedus.** He has **hastam magnam.** He throws **hastam** at **sagittarius, sed sagittarius** blocks it with his **scutum**. Then **malus dominus** rushes toward the **sagittarius** with his **gladius magnus**. The **sagittarius** has **gladium, sed** his **gladius est parvus, et** it breaks. **Sed** just before **malus dominus** strikes the final blow, **sagittarius sicam occupat et** kills **malum dominum**. Now **puella parva est** safe, **et sagittarius puellam portat** back to **oppidum**.

112 | Paideia Latina, Level A

WEEK 18: Accusative Case Continued; Second Conjugation Verbs

Goals: Translate plural direct objects in sentences and conjugate and translate second conjugation verbs.

Vocabulary

hábeo, habēre, hábui, hábitum HA-bay-oh, ha-BAY-ray, HA-boo-ee, HA-bee-toom	I have, to have, I had, had
móveo, movēre, móvi, mótum MOH-vay-oh, moh-VAY-ray, MOH-vee, MOH-toom	I move, to move, I moved, moved
órno, ornáre, ornávi, ornátum OR-noh, or-NAH-ray, or-NAH-vee, or-NAH-toom	I decorate, to decorate, I decorated, decorated
sédeo, sedēre, sédi, séssum SEH-day-oh, seh-DAY-ray, SEH-dee, SEH-soom	I sit, to sit, I sat, sat
téneo, tenēre, ténui, téntum TEH-nay-oh, teh-NAY-ray, TEH-noo-ee, TEN-toom	I hold, to hold, I held, held
vídeo, vidēre, vídi, vísum VEE-day-oh, vee-DAY-ray, VEE-dee, VEE-soom	I see, to see, I saw, seen
árgentum, árgenti (n.) AR-jen-toom, AR-jen-tee	silver
áurum, áuri (n.) OW-room, OW-ree	gold
gémma, gémmae (f.) JEM-mah, JEM-may	gem
margaríta, margarítae (f.) mar-gah-REE-tah, mar-gah-REE-tay	pearl

Highlight Masculine nouns with blue, Feminine with pink, and Neuter with yellow.

Chant: Present Tense Verb Video

	Singular	**English**	**Plural**	**English**
1st Person	video	I see	videmus	we see
2nd Person	vides	you see	videtis	y'all see
3rd Person	videt	he/she/it sees	vident	they see

Grammar Lesson

This week we learn about second conjugation verbs. A conjugation is a group of verbs that have similar stems. There are four conjugations of verbs in Latin. The first conjugation, which we already know, contains verbs whose stems end in "a".

    amo, amare → Stem = ama-

    narro, narrare → Stem = narra-

In the second conjugation, the stem of the verb ends in a long "e".

    video, vidēre → Stem = vidē-

    habeo, habēre → Stem = habē-

Once you find the stem, you can attach our normal present tense verb endings to it (-o, -s, -t, -mus, -tis, -nt). Notice that for the 1st/Sg, the -o ending does not swallow up the "e" like it does to the "a" in the first conjugation.

Grammar Sound Off

A group of verbs that have similar stems…	…is called a conjugation.
First conjugation is a group of verbs…	…whose stems end in "a."
Second conjugation is a group of verbs…	…whose stems end in long "e."

WEEK 18: Worksheet   Nomen: _____

Vocabulary: Fill in the missing parts in English and in Latin.

habeo	habēre		
		I had	

moveo			
	to move		

		ornavi	
	to decorate		

	sedēre		
			sat

teneo			
		I held	

		vidi	
			seen

| argentum | argenti | n. | |

| aurum | | | |

| | gemmae | | |

| | | | pearl |

Chants: Fill in the blanks.

"habeo, habēre, habui, habitum" is which conjugation? _____				
	Singular	**English**	**Plural**	**English**
1st Person	habe-o	I have		
2nd Person				
3rd Person				

"orno, ornare, ornavi, ornatum" is which conjugation? _____				
	Singular	**English**	**Plural**	**English**
1st Person				
2nd Person				
3rd Person	orna-t	he decorates		

"moveo, movēre, movi, motum" is which conjugation? _____				
	Singular	**English**	**Plural**	**English**
1st Person				
2nd Person				
3rd Person			move-nt	they move

Grammar: Fill in the blanks with info from your grammar and grammar sound-off from this week or from previous weeks.

1. A _____ is a group of verbs that have similar stems.
2. First conjugation verbs have stems that end in _____.
3. Second conjugation verbs have stems that end in _____ _____.
4. The _____ _____ receives the action of the verb.
5. We use the _____ case for the direct object.

Cases: Give just the Nominative and Accusative case endings.

	Masculine Singular	Feminine Singular	Neuter Singular	Masculine Plural	Feminine Plural	Neuter Plural
Nominative						
Accusative						

Changing Cases: Take each nominative noun and change it into the accusative case. If the nominative is plural, make it plural in the accusative.

feminae → feminas   equus → equum

1. margarita _____
2. margaritae _____
3. gemma   _____
4. gemmae   _____
5. scutum   _____
6. scuta   _____
7. gladius   _____
8. gladii   _____
9. sagittae   _____
10. oppida   _____
11. tumuli   _____
12. aurigae   _____

Verb Stems: Find the present stem of each verb by chopping the "-re" off the Infinitive.

video, vidēre, vidi, visum → stem = vidē

1. habeo, habēre, habui, habitum → stem = _____
2. moveo, movēre, movi, motum → stem = _____
3. orno, ornare, ornavi, ornatum → stem = _____
4. rogo, rogare, rogavi, rogatum → stem = _____
5. teneo, tenēre, tenui, tentum → stem = _____
6. sedeo, sedēre, sedi, sessum → stem = _____

Creating Verbs: Translate by finding the verb stem and then adding the correct ending.

> you all see = vide-tis
> 1. we move = _____
> 2. they have = _____
> 3. he decorates = _____
> 4. you sit = _____
> 5. she sees = _____
> 6. we hold = _____
> 7. you all move = _____
> 8. they hold = _____

Translation: Translate each sentence into English. Watch out for plural DO's!

1. Tabernarius margaritas movet.

_____

2. Sagittarius sagittas videt.

_____

3. Aurigae scuta tenent.

_____

4. Sicas habemus.

_____

5. Nautae gladios occupant.

_____

Fabula: Read the story below. (You do not have to write anything down.)

Tabernarius et Margaritae

Tabernarius tabernam habet near **forum. Tabernarius sedet in tabernā** all day and waits for **viri et feminae intrare tabernam. In tabernā sunt margaritae et gemmae. Aurum in tabernā est, et argentum. Tabernarius gemmas ornat** with **aurum et argentum. Tabernarius movet gemmas** near **fenestra** so that **viri et feminae vident** when **ambulant** by **taberna in viā.**

Femina pulchra ianuam of **taberna intrat. Femina margaritas videt.** "How much **sunt margaritae tuae?" femina rogat. Tabernarius narrat magna** price to **femina. Femina aurum videt, argentum videt, gemmas videt. Sed femina margaritas amat. Femina margaritas tenet** in her hands. "**Non habeo** that much money," **femina narrat. Tabernarius narrat parva** price to **femina. Femina est dubia, sed margaritas amat. Femina dat** money to **tabernarius. Tabernarius dat margaritas** to **femina.**

Femina est laeta! Femina margaritas pulchras habet. Tabernarius est laetus. Tabernarius money **habet. Sed tabernarius est** also **laetus** because he knows that **margaritae non sunt verae margaritae. Margaritae sunt falsae et tabernarius est falsus!**

WEEK 19: Imperfect Tense

Goals: Chant the imperfect endings and translate imperfect verbs.

Vocabulary

desídero, desideráre, desiderávi, desiderátum day-SEE-day-roh, day-see-day-RAH-ray, day-see-day-RAH-vee, day-see-day-RAH-toom	I desire, to desire, I desired, desired
láudo, laudáre, laudávi, laudátum LAHW-doh, lahw-DAH-ray, lahw-DAH-vee, lahw-DAH-toom	I praise, to praise, I praised, praised
néco, necáre, necávi, necátum NEH-coh, neh-CAH-ray, neh-CAH-vee, neh-CAH-toom	I kill, to kill, I killed, killed
oppúgno, oppugnáre, oppugnávi, oppugnátum oh-POOG-noh, oh-poog-NAH-ray, oh-poog-NAH-vee, oh-poog-NAH-toom	I attack, to attack, I attacked, attacked
púgno, pugnáre, pugnávi, pugnátum POOG-noh, poog-NAH-ray, poog-NAH-vee, poog-NAH-toom	I fight, to fight, I fought, fought
númquam NOOM-quahm	never
sáepe SAY-pay	often
sémper SEM-per	always

Chant: Imperfect Tense Verb Endings

	Singular	Plural
1st Person	-bam	-bamus
2nd Person	-bas	-batis
3rd Person	-bat	-bant

Chant: Imperfect Tense Verb Amo

	Singular	English	Plural	English
1st Person	amabam	I was loving	amabamus	we were loving
2nd Person	amabas	you were loving	amabatis	y'all were loving
3rd Person	amabat	he was loving	amabant	they were loving

Chant: Imperfect Tense Verb Video

	Singular	English	Plural	English
1st Person	videbam	I was seeing	videbamus	we were seeing
2nd Person	videbas	you were seeing	videbatis	y'all were seeing
3rd Person	videbat	he was seeing	videbant	they were seeing

Grammar Lesson

Besides having person and number, verbs also have tense. **Tense** means what time the verb is happening. The three basic tenses are present (happening now), future (happening later), and past (already happened). Latin has two different past tenses, the imperfect tense and the perfect tense. This week we will learn the imperfect tense.

The **imperfect tense** refers to an action that was going on for a period of time in the past. *He was working. She was praying. They were walking.* To translate the imperfect tense, use the helping verbs "was" or "were".

To form the imperfect tense, we simply take the present stem (which we find by chopping off the "-re" from the infinitive, and adding the endings: -bam, -bas, -bat, -bamus, -batis, -bant. You'll notice that all the endings have a "-ba-" in them, and that they mostly end in the same way as the present tense endings.

Grammar Sound Off

A verb is an action…	…or a state of being.
Each verb has…	…four principal parts:
Present, Infinitive, Perfect…	…Passive Participle or Supine.
We get the present stem…	…from the Infinitive.
To get the present stem…	…chop off the R E.

What is the tense?	**When** did it happen?
The three basic tenses…	…are Present, Imperfect, Future.
The Present tense…	…is happening now.
The Imperfect tense…	…was happening in the past.
First Person Singular…	…-bam, -bam, -bam…I was, I was
Second Person Singular…	…-bas, -bas, -bas…you were, you were
Third Person Singular…	…-bat, -bat, -bat…he, she, it was
First Person Plural…	…-bamus, -bamus, -bamus…we were, we were
Second Person Plural…	…-batis, -batis, -batis…y'all were, y'all were
Third Person Plural…	…-bant, -bant, -bant…they were, they were

MYTHOLOGY

Vesta was the goddess of the home and the hearth (the fireplace that kept the house warm). Her Greek name was **Hestia**. Her temple in the Roman forum was cared for by special priestesses called Vestal Virgins whose job was to never let the sacred fire go out.

122 | Paideia Latina, Level A

WEEK 19: Worksheet   Nomen: _____

Vocabulary: Fill in the missing parts in English and in Latin.

desidero	desiderare		

			laudatum

		necavi	
	to kill		

	oppugnare		

pugno			
		I fought	

numquam	

saepe	

	Always

Are the verbs in this vocabulary list first conjugation or second conjugation? (HINT: Look at the vowel the verb stem ends in.) _____

Chants: Fill in the blanks.

	Present Tense of "neco, necare, necavi, necatum"			
	Singular	**English**	**Plural**	**English**
1st	neco	I kill		
2nd				
3rd				

	Imperfect Tense of "neco, necare, necavi, necatum"			
	Singular	**English**	**Plural**	**English**
1st	necabam	I was killing		
2nd				
3rd				

	Imperfect Tense of "sedeo, sedēre, sedi, sessum"			
	Singular	**English**	**Plural**	**English**
1st	sedebam	I was sitting		
2nd				
3rd				

Grammar: Fill in the blanks with info from your grammar and grammar sound-off from this week or from previous weeks.

1. A verb's tense tells us _____ the verb happens.
2. The three basic tenses in Latin are _____, _____, and _____.
3. We use "was" or "were" to translate the _____ tense.

Matching: Draw a straight line matching up the verb endings on each side with the person and number in the middle.

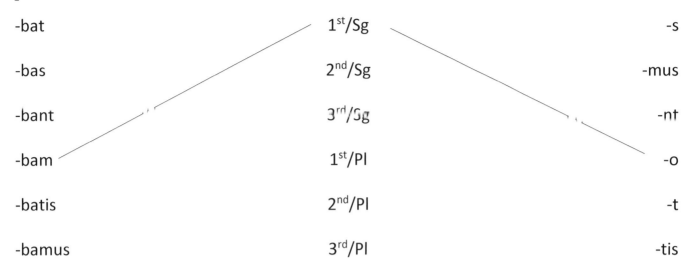

-bat	1st/Sg	-s
-bas	2nd/Sg	-mus
-bant	3rd/Sg	-nt
-bam	1st/Pl	-o
-batis	2nd/Pl	-t
-bamus	3rd/Pl	-tis

Parsing Verbs: Find the Person, Number, and Tense of each verb and then translate into Latin.

	pugna-bas	2nd/Sg/Imp	you were fighting
1.	pugna-bant	___/___/___	_____
2.	pugna-nt	___/___/___	_____
3.	neca-bamus	___/___/___	_____
4.	desidera-t	___/___/___	_____
5.	oppugna-batis	___/___/___	_____
6.	lauda-bat	___/___/___	_____
7.	neca-bam	___/___/___	_____

Derivatives: Answer these questions about derivatives.

1. *Pugnacious* comes from the Latin "pugno." A pugnacious person is someone who is always ready to get in a _____.

2. We give God all glory, laud, and honor. Another word for *laud* is _____.

3. The motto of the Coast Guard is "Semper Paratus" which means _____ _____.

4. Ornate comes from the Latin "orno." If a picture frame is ornate, it is very _____.

5. "Teneo" means "I hold." An octopus holds things with its _____.

6. The word *occupy* comes from "Occupo." If an army occupies an enemy city, then the army _____ the city.

7. Since *gladiator* comes from the Latin "gladius," it's likely that a Roman gladiator would have a _____ for a weapon.

Fabula: Read the story below. (You do not have to write anything down.)

Pulchra Helena

History books **semper narrant fabulam** about **Helena** of Troy. **Helena est regina** of Sparta in the **patria** Greece. **Helena est** the most **pulchra femina** in the world. Paris, prince of Troy, **desiderabat Helenam**. Paris **navigabat** to Sparta **et occupabat Helenam**. Paris **navigabat** with Helena to Troy. Menelaus, the husband of Helena, **est iratus**. Menelaus **vocabat** his **germanum et amicos** in Greece. **Navigabant** to Troy to get Helen back. The Greeks and Trojans **pugnabant** for nine years. The Greeks **saepe oppugnabant** Troy, **sed numquam victoriam habebant**. Finally, the Greeks **aedificabant** a wooden **equum**. **Viri** hide inside **equus**. The Trojans **equum portabant** into **oppidum**. At night, the Greeks came out of the wooden **equus, et necabant** the Trojans. The Greeks **Helenam occupabant, et navigabant** back to Greece.

WEEK 20: Imperfect Tense Continued

Goal: Translate imperfect verbs in sentences.

Vocabulary

áro, aráre, arávi, arátum AH-roh, ah-RAH-ray, ah-RAH-vee, ah-RAH-toom	I plow, to plow, I plowed, plowed
céno, cenáre, cenávi, cenátum CHAY-noh, chay-NAH-ray, chay-NAH-vee, chay-NAH-toom	I dine, to dine, I dined, dined
demónstro, demonstráre, demonstrávi, demonstrátum day-MON-stroh, day-mon-STRAH-ray, day-mon-STRAH-vee, day-mon-STRAH-toom	I point out, to point out, I pointed out, pointed out
hábito, habitáre, habitávi, habitátum HA-bee-toh, ha-bee-TAH-ray, ha-bee-TAH-vee, ha-bee-TAH-toom	I live, to live, I lived, lived
póto, potáre, potávi, potátum POH-toh, poh-TAH-ray, poh-TAH-vee, poh-TAH-toom	I drink, to drink, I drank, drunk
dum DOOM	while
nunc NOONC	now
tunc TOONC	then

Grammar Lesson & Sound Off

Review last week's lesson and sound off.

WEEK 20: Worksheet   Nomen: _____

Vocabulary: Fill in the missing parts in English and in Latin.

aro		aravi	

			cenatum
I dine			

		demonstravi	
	to point out		

habito			

	potare		
	to drink		

dum	

	now

	then

Are the verbs in this vocabulary list first conjugation or second conjugation? (HINT: Look at the vowel the verb stem ends in.) _____

128 | Paideia Latina, Level A

Chants: Fill in the blanks.

Present Tense of "poto, potare, potavi, potatum"				
	Singular	English	Plural	English
1st	poto	I drink		
2nd				
3rd				

Imperfect Tense of "poto, potare, potavi, potatum"				
	Singular	English	Plural	English
1st				
2nd				
3rd			potabant	they were drinking

Tense Swap: Change each Present tense verb to Imperfect tense keeping the same Person and Number and translate.

ara-nt → ara-bant = they were plowing

1. habita-s → _____ = _____

2. pota-t → _____ = _____

3. cena-mus → _____ = _____

4. demonstr-o → _____ = _____

5. ara-tis → _____ = _____

Word Hunt: Choose the <u>best</u> word from the box to put in each of the sentences below.

aro	ceno	demonstro	habito	poto
desidero	laudo	neco	oppugno	pugno

1. If I am a farmer, _____ my fields.
2. If I am Santa Claus, _____ at the North Pole.
3. If I am thirsty, _____ water.
4. If I am Cain, _____ Abel.
5. If I sing in church, _____ God.
6. If I am a Greek, _____ the city of Troy.
7. If I go to a restaurant, _____ on my favorite food.
8. If I put something on my wish list, _____ it.
9. If I am a superhero, _____ villains.
10. If I see a mistake, _____ it to the teacher.

Translation: Translate the sentences into English. Be careful to translate your verbs in the imperfect tense and watch out for direct objects!

1. Lauda<u>bam</u> poet**am**.

_____

2. Auriga saepe oppugna<u>bat</u>.

_____

3. Femina margarit**as** semper desidera<u>bat</u>.

_____

4. Tunc nautae urs**am** neca<u>bant</u>.

_____

5. Elephantus camel**um** nunc pugna<u>bat</u>.

_____

6. Demonstra**batis** aur**um** et argent**um**.

7. Magistra discipul**um** stult**um** numquam lauda**bat**.

8. Sagittarius in silvā habita**bat**.

9. Femina aqu**am** pota**bat**, sed vir vin**um** pota**bat**.

10. Agricola agr**os** ara**bat** dum dominus cena**bat**.

11. Agricolae arabant, nautae navigabant, poetae cantabant, et ventus flabat.

Fabula: Read the story below. (You do not have to write anything down.)

Aqua et Vinum

Christus was born in Bethlehem, **et habitabat** in **patria** Judea. **Christus non est agricola, et non arabat agros. Christus est** carpenter. **Christus est filius** of **Deus, et dum Christus est** on **terra**, he does miracles.

Christus est at a wedding **cena** with **Maria**, his mother. **Feminae et viri sedebant** at **magnae mensae. Dominus** of the feast **sedebat** at the head of the **mensa. Cenabant, et vinum potabant. Nunc, est** no more **vinum. Maria demonstrabat** this to **Christus. Tunc, Christus narrabat servos** to put **aquam** in large jars. **Dum servi** obey **Christum, aqua** turns into **vinum. Viri et feminae vinum novum potabant. Viri et feminae sunt laeti. Narrabant dominum** of the feast, "You have saved **bonum vinum** for last."

WEEK 21: REVIEW

Goals: Retain and recall vocabulary and grammar from weeks 17-20.

Vocabulary

Check off the ones you know.

- ☐ **argentum** — silver
- ☐ **aro** — I plow
- ☐ **aurum** — gold
- ☐ **ceno** — I dine
- ☐ **demonstro** — I point out
- ☐ **desidero** — I desire
- ☐ **dum** — while
- ☐ **galea** — helmet
- ☐ **gemma** — gem
- ☐ **gladius** — sword
- ☐ **habeo** — I have
- ☐ **habito** — I live
- ☐ **harena** — sand
- ☐ **hasta** — spear
- ☐ **laudo** — I praise+
- ☐ **linea** — line, string
- ☐ **margarita** — pearl
- ☐ **moveo** — I move
- ☐ **neco** — I kill
- ☐ **numquam** — never
- ☐ **nunc** — now
- ☐ **occupo** — I seize
- ☐ **oppugno** — I attack
- ☐ **orno** — I decorate
- ☐ **poto** — I drink
- ☐ **pugno** — I fight
- ☐ **saepe** — often
- ☐ **sagitta** — arrow
- ☐ **sagittarius** — archer
- ☐ **scutum** — shield
- ☐ **sedeo** — I sit
- ☐ **semper** — always
- ☐ **sica** — dagger
- ☐ **teneo** — I hold
- ☐ **tunc** — then
- ☐ **victoria** — victory
- ☐ **video** — I see

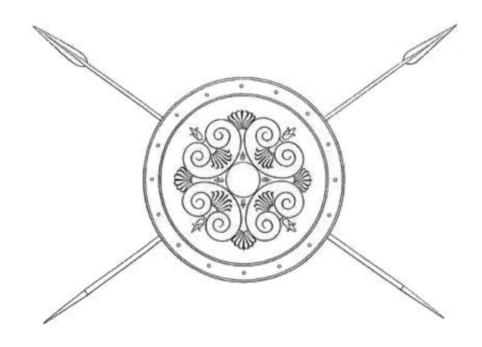

132 | Paideia Latina, Level A

WEEK 21: Review Worksheet   Nomen: _____

Cases: Give just the Nominative and Accusative case endings.

	Masculine Singular	Feminine Singular	Neuter Singular	Masculine Plural	Feminine Plural	Neuter Plural
Nominative						
Accusative						

Verbs: Fill in the empty boxes.

Present Tense of "moveo, movēre, movi, motum"				
	Singular	English	Plural	English
1st				
2nd				
3rd	move-t	he moves		

Imperfect Tense of "moveo, movēre, movi, motum"				
	Singular	English	Plural	English
1st				
2nd			move-batis	y'all were moving
3rd				

Tense Swap: Change the present verbs into imperfect, keeping the same person and number, and then translate.

    ama-s → ama-bas = you were loving

1. habe-nt → _____ = _____
2. orna-mus → _____ = _____

Paideia Latina, Level A | 133

Vocabulary: Fill in the crossword puzzle with vocabulary from chapters 17-20.

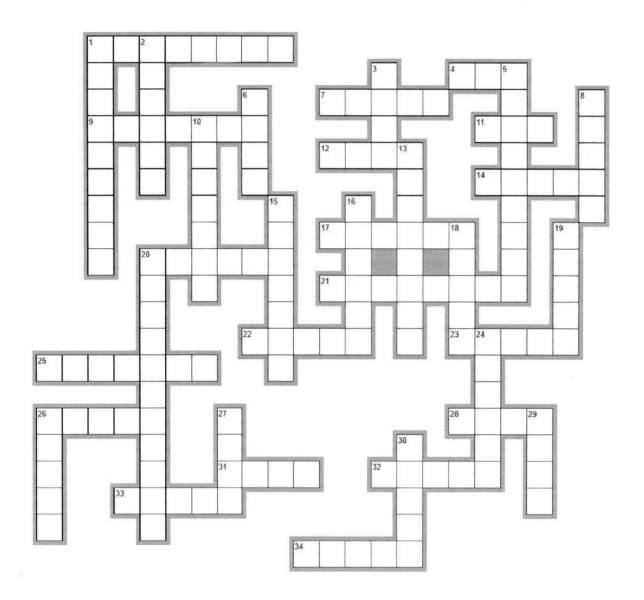

Word Bank

ARGENTUM	ARO	AURUM	CENO	DEMONSTRO	DESIDERO	DUM	GALEA	GEMMA
GLADIUS	HABEO	HABITO	HARENA	HASTA	LAUDO	LINEA	MARGARITA	MOVEO	NECO
NUMQUAM	NUNC	OCCUPO	OPPUGNO	ORNO	POTO	PUGNO	SAEPE	SAGITTA
SAGITTARIUS	SCUTUM	SEDEO	SEMPER	SICA	TENEO	TUNC	VICTORIA	VIDEO

Across

1. I desire
4. while
7. I praise
9. I attack
11. I plow
12. dagger
14. often
17. sand
20. shield
21. victory
22. I have
23. I move
25. arrow
26. helmet
28. then
31. I kill
32. I see
33. I fight
34. spear

Down

1. I point out
2. always
3. now
5. pearl
6. I drink
8. I sit
10. sword
13. silver
15. never
16. I live
18. gold
19. I hold
20. archer
24. I seize
26. gem
27. I decorate
29. I dine
30. line, string

Chant: Fill in the blanks using the word "boy."

CASE	JOB	Singular	Plural
Nominative		the *boy*	
	IO		

Grammar: Fill in the blanks with info from your grammar sound offs.

1. A _____ _____ receives action from the verb.
2. We use the _____ case for the direct object.
3. In the _____ gender, the nominative and accusative cases look the same.
4. A verb's tense tells us _____ the verb happens.
5. The three basic tenses in Latin are _____, _____, and _____.
6. We use "was" or "were" to translate the _____ tense.

Changing Cases: Take each nominative noun and change it into the accusative. If the nominative is plural, make it plural in the accusative.

feminae → feminas   equus → equum

1. linea   _____   6. scuta   _____
2. lineae   _____   7. sagittarius _____
3. sagitta _____   8. sagittarii _____
4. sagittae _____   9. sicae   _____
5. scutum   _____   10. equi   _____

Translation: Translate each sentence into Latin.

> EXAMPLE: The archer was seizing the string.
>
> __sagittari-us__   __line-am__   __occupa-bat__
> Nom/Sg/Masc.   Acc/Sg/Fem.   Verb Stem + Imp/ 3rd/Sg

1. The shopkeeper was giving false pearls.

   _____ _____ _____ _____
   Nom/Sg/Masc   Acc/**Pl**/Fem   Acc/**Pl**/Fem   Verb Stem + Imp/3rd/Sg

2. The large sailor was holding the helmet.

   _____ _____ _____ _____
   Nom/Sg/Masc*   Nom/Sg /Masc   Acc/Sg/Fem   Verb Stem + Imp/3rd/Sg

3. We were attacking the small towns.

   _____ _____ _____
   Acc/**Pl**/Neut   Acc/**Pl**/Neut   Verb Stem + Imp/1st/**Pl**

4. The boys see gold and silver.

   _____ _____ ___ _____ _____
   Nom/**Pl**/Masc   Acc/Sg/Neut   Acc/Sg/Neut   Verb Stem +Pres/3rd/**Pl**

Translation: Translate each sentence into English.

1. Femina aurum, et argentum, et margaritas semper laudabat.

   _____

2. Sagittarius gemmas in harenā demonstrabat.

   _____

3. Nunc Christus victoriam habet, et Christum habemus.

   _____

4. Sedebam et vinum potabam, sed stabas et aquam potabas.

   _____

WEEK 22: Future Tense

Goals: Chant the future endings and translate future verbs.

Vocabulary

	créo, creáre, creávi, creátum CRAY-oh, cray-AH-ray, cray-AH-vee, cray-AH-toom	I create, to create, I created, created
	plóro, ploráre, plorávi, plorátum PLOH-roh, ploh-RAH-ray, ploh-RAH-vee, ploh-RAH-toom	I cry, to cry, I cried, cried
	spécto, spectáre, spectávi, spectátum SPEC-toh, spec-TAH-ray, spec-TAH-vee, spec-TAH-toom	I look at, to look at, I looked at, seen
	tárdo, tardáre, tardávi, tardátum TAR-doh, tar-DAH-ray, tar-DAH-vee, tar-DAH-toom	I delay, to delay, I delayed, delayed
	vérbero, verberáre, verberávi, verberátum VER-ber-oh, ver-ber-AH-ray, ver-ber-AH-vee, ver-ber-AH-toom	I beat, to beat, I beat, beaten
	hódie HO-dee-ay	today
	héri HAIR-ee	yesterday
	crás cross	tomorrow

MYTHOLOGY

Mercury, whose Greek names was **Hermes,** was the god of messages, money, travelers, and trickery. He wore winged sandals on his feet and delivered Jupiter's messages to both gods and humans.

Chant: Future Tense Verb Endings

	Singular	Plural
1st Person	-bo	-bimus
2nd Person	-bis	-bitis
3rd Person	-bit	-bunt

Chant: Future Tense Verb Amo

	Singular	English	Plural	English
1st	amabo	I will love	amabimus	we will love
2nd	amabis	you will love	amabitis	y'all will love
3rd	amabit	he will love	amabunt	they will love

Chant: Future Tense Verb Video

	Singular	English	Plural	English
1st	videbo	I will see	videbimus	we will see
2nd	videbis	you will see	videbitis	y'all will see
3rd	videbit	he will see	videbunt	they will see

Grammar Lesson

We already learned that three basic verb tenses are present (happening now), future (happening later), and past (already happened). This week we will focus on future tense.

The **future tense** refers to an action that has not yet happened. *He will work. She will pray. They will create.* To translate the future tense, use the helping verb "will."

To form the future tense, we simply take the present stem (which we find by chopping off the "-re" from the infinitive) and add the endings: -bo, -bis, -bit, -bimus, -bitis, -bunt. You'll notice that most of the endings have a "-bi-" in them. In the first person singular, the "-o" swallows up the "i" of the "-bi-" and it becomes "-bo." In the third person plural, the "i" changes to a "u" before the "-nt."

Grammar Sound Off

A verb is an action…	…or a state of being.
Each verb has…	…four principal parts:
Present, Infinitive, Perfect…	…Passive Participle or Supine.
We get the present stem…	…from the Infinitive.
To get the present stem…	…chop off the R E.
What is the tense?	<u>When</u> did it happen?
The three basic tenses…	…are Present, Imperfect, Future.
The Present tense…	…is happening now.
The Imperfect tense…	…was happening in the past.
The Future tense…	…will happen in the future.
First Person Singular…	…-bo, -bo, -bo…I will be, I will be
Second Person Singular…	…-bis, -bis, -bis…you will be, you will be
Third Person Singular…	…-bit, -bit, -bit…he will be, she will be
First Person Plural…	…-bimus, -bimus, -bimus…we will be, we will be
Second Person Plural…	…-bitis, -bitis, -bitis…y'all will be, y'all will be
Third Person Plural…	…-bunt, -bunt, -bunt…they will be, they will be

Mythology

Vulcan was the god of fire and metalworking. His Greek name was **Hephaestus**. During the siege of Troy, Vulcan made a famous suit of armor for the hero Achilles. He also was responsible for making Jupiter's thunderbolts. We get the word "volcano" from this god.

WEEK 22: Worksheet   Nomen: _____

Vocabulary: Fill in the missing parts in English and in Latin.

creo		creavi	

			ploratum
I cry			

		spectavi	
		I looked at	

tardo			

	verberare		

hodie	

heri	

	tomorrow

Are the verbs in this vocabulary list first conjugation or second conjugation? (HINT: Look at the vowel the verb stem ends in.) _____

Chants: Fill in the blanks.

	Present Tense of "creo, creare, creavi, creatum"			
	Singular	**English**	**Plural**	**English**
1st	creo	I create		
2nd				
3rd				

	Imperfect Tense of "creo, creare, creavi, creatum"			
	Singular	**English**	**Plural**	**English**
1st	crea-bam	I was creating		
2nd				
3rd				

	Future Tense of "creo, creare, creavi, creatum"			
	Singular	**English**	**Plural**	**English**
1st	crea-bo	I will create		
2nd				
3rd				

Translation: Translate these future tense verbs into English.

1. verbera-bis = _____
2. plora-bit = _____
3. crea-bitis = _____
4. specta-bunt = _____
5. tarda-bo = _____

Matching: Draw a straight line matching up the verb endings on each side with the person and number in the middle.

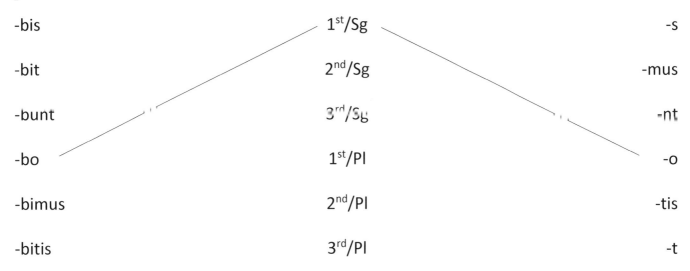

Word Hunt: Choose the best word from the box to put in each of the sentences below.

creo	ploro	specto	tardo	verbero
hodie	heri	cras		

1. If I skin my knee, _____.
2. _____ the carpet with a stick to get the dirt out.
3. _____ myself in the mirror.
4. Jesus said not to worry about what _____ will bring. The cares of _____ are enough.
5. _____ comes before today.
6. If _____ on each problem, I will not have enough time to pass the math drill.
7. _____ new things because I am made in God's image.

Paideia Latina, Level A | 143

Time: Look at the tense of the verb and circle whether these things happened "heri" (yesterday), "hodie" (today), or "cras" (tomorrow).

Marcus was plowing the field ((heri) / hodie / cras).

1. Marcus is fighting the wolf (heri / hodie / cras).
2. Quintus will create a table (heri / hodie / cras).
3. Flavius was crying in the forest (heri / hodie / cras).
4. The brothers were looking at the camel (heri / hodie / cras).
5. The queens will carry the gems (heri / hodie / cras).

Translation: Translate the sentences into English. Be careful to translate your verbs in the future tense!

1. Scriba servum malum verberabit.

   _____

2. Cibum in culinā creabimus.

   _____

3. Regina pulchra castellum cras spectabit.

   _____

4. Puellae parvae in silvā plorabunt.

   _____

5. Amicus meus tardabit et plorabo.

   _____

Fabula: Read the story below. (You do not have to write anything down.)

A Birthday for **Meus Filius**

Cras est birthday of **meus filius. Parabo** for his birthday. **Creabo** cake. **Flabo** balloons. **Amici casam intrabunt. Amici dona magna** to **meus filius dabunt. Cenabimus, potabimus, et verberabimus** pinata. If **tardabimus habēre** dessert, **meus filius plorabit. Meus puer parvus amat** cake! **Hodie meus filius est** one year old, **sed cras** he will be two years old.

WEEK 23: Present, Imperfect, and Future Tenses

Goal: Do a verb synopsis in present, imperfect, and future tenses.

Vocabulary

dóceo, docēre, dócui, dóctum DOH-chay-oh, doh-CHAY-ray, DOH-coo-ee, DOHC-toom	I teach, to teach, I taught, taught
gáudeo, gaudēre, gavísus sum, --- GAHW-day-oh, gahw-DAY-ray, gah-VEE-soos SOOM	I rejoice, to rejoice, I rejoiced
iáceo, iacēre, iácui, --- YAH-chay-oh, yah-CHAY-ray, YAH-coo-ee	I lie down, to lie down, I lay down
iúbeo, iubēre, iússi, iússum YOO-bay-oh, yoo-BAY-ray, YOO-see, YOO-soom	I order, to order, I ordered, ordered
móneo, monēre, mónui, mónitum MOH-nay-oh, moh-NAY-ray, MOH-noo-ee, MOH-nee-toom	I warn, to warn, I warned, warned
ánnus, ánni (m.) AH-noose, AH-nee	year
hóra, hórae (f.) HOH-rah, HOH-ray	hour
vérbum, vérbi (n.) VAIR-boom, VAIR-bee	word

Highlight Masculine nouns with blue, Feminine with pink, and Neuter with yellow.

Chant: Present, Imperfect, Future Verb Endings

	Present	Imperfect	Future
1st/Sg	-o	-bam	-bo
2nd/Sg	-s	-bas	-bis
3rd/Sg	-t	-bat	-bit
1st/Pl	-mus	-bamus	-bimus
2nd/Pl	-tis	-batis	-bitis
3rd/Pl	-nt	-bant	-bunt

Grammar Lesson

Now that we know the present, imperfect, and future tenses, we can do a verb synopsis. A **verb synopsis** is where you take a verb in a certain person and number and put it through all the different tenses.

	Verb Synopsis of "Amo, Amare, Amavi, Amatum" in the 1st/Pl	
	Latin	*English*
Present	ama-mus	we love
Imperfect	ama-bamus	we were loving
Future	ama-bimus	we will love

	Verb Synopsis of "Video, Vidēre, Vidi, Visum" in the 3rd/Pl	
	Latin	*English*
Present	vide-nt	they see
Imperfect	vide-bant	they were seeing
Future	vide-bunt	they will see

Grammar Sound Off

A group of verbs that have similar stems…	…is called a conjugation.
First conjugation is a group of verbs…	…whose stems end in "a."
Second conjugation is a group of verbs…	…whose stems end in long "e."
A verb synopsis takes a verb…	*…and puts it through the different tenses.*
First person singular…	*…-o, -bam, -bo*
Second person singular…	*…-s, -bas, -bis*
Third person singular…	*…-t, -bat, -bit*
First person plural…	*…-mus, -bamus, -bimus*
Second person plural…	*…-tis, -batis, -bitis*
Third person plural…	*…-nt, -bant, -bunt*

WEEK 23: Worksheet   Nomen: _____

Vocabulary: Fill in the missing parts in English and in Latin.

doceo		docui	
			taught

gaudeo		gavisus sum	
	to rejoice		

iaceo			
		I lay down	

iubeo			

	monēre		

annus		m.	

			hour

			word

Are the verbs in this vocabulary list first conjugation or second conjugation? (HINT: Look at the vowel the verb stem ends in.) _____

Chants: Fill in the blanks.

	Present	Imperfect	Future
1st/Sg	-o	-bam	-bo
2nd/Sg			
3rd/Sg			
1st/Pl			
2nd/Pl			
3rd/Pl			

	Verb Synopsis of "Amo, Amare, Amavi, Amatum" in the 2nd/Sg	
	Latin	English
Present	ama-s	
Imperfect		
Future		

	Verb Synopsis of "iubeo, iubēre, iussi, iussum" in the 3rd/Sg	
	Latin	English
Present	iube-t	
Imperfect		
Future		

	Verb Synopsis of "gaudeo, gaudēre, gavisus sum" in the 3rd/Pl	
	Latin	English
Present	gaude-nt	
Imperfect		
Future		

Translation: Translate these verbs into English. Watch out! They could be present, imperfect, or future tense.

1. gaude-tis _____
2. mone-bant _____
3. verbera-s _____
4. iace-bit _____
5. iube-bam _____
6. doce-bunt _____
7. plora-mus _____
8. tarda-nt _____
9. crea-bitis _____
10. specta-bo _____

Time: Circle whether each activity would take an "annus" (year) or a "hora" (hour).

Folding three loads of laundry. (annus /(hora))

1. Growing three inches taller. (annus / hora)
2. Baking a cake. (annus / hora)
3. Walking across the United States. (annus / hora)
4. Cleaning your room. (annus / hora)
5. Learning a foreign language. (annus / hora)

Derivatives: Answer these questions about derivatives.

1. *Annual* comes from "annus." An annual event happens once every _____.

2. *Verbose* comes from "verbum." A verbose person speaks a lot of _____.

3. *Admonish* comes from "moneo." If your parents admonish you, they are giving you a _____.

4. *Spectator* comes from "specto." A spectator is someone who _____ an event.

Translation: Translate each sentence into Latin.

EXAMPLE: The teacher will warn the student.		
__magistr-a__	__discipul-um__	__mone-bit__
Nom/Sg/Fem.	Acc/Sg/Masc.	Verb Stem + Fut/ 3rd/Sg

1. The happy women will rejoice.

   _____   _____   _____
   Nom/**Pl**/Fem   Nom/**Pl**/Fem   Verb Stem + Fut/3rd/**Pl**

2. The bad boy was beating the camel.

   _____   _____   _____   _____
   Nom/Sg/Masc   Nom/Sg/Masc   Acc/Sg/Masc   Verb Stem + Imp/3rd/Sg

3. You all will teach the foolish farmers.

   _____   _____   _____
   Acc/**Pl**/Masc* Acc/**Pl**/Masc Verb Stem + Fut/2nd/**Pl**

4. The shopkeeper looks at the hour.

   _____   _____   _____
   Nom/Sg/Masc   Acc/Sg/Fem   Verb Stem +Pres/3rd/Sg

Fabula: Read the story below. (You do not have to write anything down.)

The Mysterious **Verba et Stultus Vir**

Many **anni** before **Christus, stultus vir** in Babylon **habitabat**. The grandfather of **stultus vir occupabat aurum** from the Temple in Jerusalem. **Nunc, stultus vir aurum habebat et gaudebat. Hodie, stultus vir magam cenam habebat. Stultus vir cenabat** on plates from the Temple. **Stultus vir potabat** from cups from the Temple. **Viri et feminae iacebant** on couches around the **mensa magna. Horae** pass.

Tunc, a hand appears, **et** writes **verba** on **murus. Stultus vir non** understands **verba. Viri et feminae non** understand **verba. Stultus vir vocat** Daniel. Daniel **intrat et verba spectat. Stultus vir iubet** Daniel to translate **verba.** Daniel **docet verba** to **stultus vir.** "**Non es aptus** king. **Viri oppugnabunt tuum oppidum.**" **Verba stultum virum monent.** That same night, the Persians **oppugnabunt** Babylon. **Occupabunt oppidum et stultum virum necabunt.**

WEEK 24: Imperfect of Irregular Verb "Sum"

Goals: Recite "sum" in the imperfect tense and translate.

Vocabulary

accúso, accusáre, accusávi, accusátum ah-COO-soh, ah-coo-SAH-ray, ah-coo-SAH-vee, ah-coo-SAH-toom	I accuse, to accuse, I accused, accused
áltus, álta, áltum ALL-toose, ALL-tah, ALL-toom	high, deep, tall
cálidus, cálida, cálidum CAH-lee-doose, CAH-lee-dah, CAH-lee-doom	warm, hot
féssus, féssa, féssum FES-soose, FES-sah, FES-soom	tired
frígidus, frígida, frígidum FREE-jee-doose, FREE-gee-dah, FREE-gee-doom	cold
grátus, gráta, grátum GRAH-toose, GRAH-tah, GRAH-toom	grateful
horréndus, horrénda, horréndum hor-REN-doose, hor-REN-dah, hor-REN-doom	horrendous
látus, láta, látum LAH-toose, LAH-tah, LAH-toom	wide
lóngus, lónga, lóngum LON-goose, LON-gah, LON-goom	long
múltus, múlta, múltum MULL-toose, MULL-tah, MULL-toom	much (sg.), many (pl.)
sórdidus, sórdida, sórdidum SOR-dee-doose, SOR-dee-dah, SOR-dee-doom	dirty

Chant: Imperfect Tense Verb Sum

	Singular	**English**	**Plural**	**English**
1st Person	eram	I was	eramus	we were
2nd Person	eras	you were	eratis	y'all were
3rd Person	erat	he/she/it was	erant	they were

Grammar Lesson

Remember when we said that the verb, "sum, esse, fui, futurum" was an **irregular verb**? It had two stems for the present tense "su-" and "es-". And because it is irregular, it actually uses a third **different stem** for the imperfect and future tenses: "er-".

Instead of attaching the normal imperfect endings, we have slightly different imperfect endings for "sum, esse." The "b" in the ending goes away when we attach it to "er-".

er-am	**er**-amus
er-as	**er**-atis
er-at	**er**-ant

The imperfect of "sum, esse" is a **linking verb**, just like the present of that verb. It connects two Nominative nouns or adjectives together by saying that one of them *was* the other one. You can think of it as an equal sign (=).

Example: Magistra mea *erat* femina.

My teacher *was* a woman.

Grammar Sound Off

Nominative case...	...Subject Noun, SN, Predicate Nominative, PRN.
The Subject Noun...	...does the verb.
The Predicate Nominative...	...renames the subject.
They're connected...	...by a linking verb.
SN-LV-PRN...	...SN-LV-PRN

WEEK 24: Worksheet   Nomen: _____

Vocabulary: Fill in the missing parts in English and in Latin.

accuso			
			accused

| altus | alta | altum | |

| calidus | | | |

| | | | tired |

| | frigida | | |

| | | gratum | |

| | | | horrendous |

| latus | | | |

| longus | | | |

| | multa | | |

| | | | dirty |

Paideia Latina, Level A | 153

Chants: Complete the chants by filling in the empty boxes.

	Present Tense of "Sum, Esse, Fui, Futurum"			
	Singular	**English**	**Plural**	**English**
1st Person	sum	I am		
2nd Person				
3rd Person				

	Imperfect Tense of "Sum, Esse, Fui, Futurum"			
	Singular	**English**	**Plural**	**English**
1st Person	eram	I was		
2nd Person				
3rd Person				

Matching: Draw a straight line matching up the verbs on each side with the person and number in the middle.

eramus   1st/Sg ———— sum

erant   2nd/Sg   est

erat   3rd/Sg   sunt

eram   1st/Pl   estis

eratis   2nd/Pl   es

eras   3rd/Pl   sumus

Translation: Translate each verb into English.

1. eramus _____
2. eras _____
3. sunt _____
4. es _____
5. eram _____
6. eratis _____
7. sum _____
8. erat _____
9. sumus _____
10. erant _____

Plurals: Change each Nominative Singular phrase into a Nominative Plural and then translate.

linea longa → lineae longae = long strings

1. aedificium latum → _____ = _____
2. harena calida → _____ = _____
3. fluvius frigidus → _____ = _____
4. magistra fessa → _____ = _____
5. lupus horrendus → _____ = _____
6. aqua alta → _____ = _____
7. amicus gratus → _____ = _____
8. vinum multum → _____ = _____
9. sella sordida → _____ = _____

Picturae: Draw a picture to illustrate each sentence below.

| Hasta erat longa. | Vir erat latus. |

Translation: Translate each sentence into English.

1. Sum grata hodie, sed eram horrenda heri.

2. Femina erat frigida, sed vir erat calidus.

3. Aedificia multa erant longa et lata et alta.

4. "Eratis sordidi discipuli," magistra accusabat.

5. Heri eramus fessi dum errabamus in silvā calidā.

Fabula: Read the story below. (You do not have to write anything down.)

Casa in Silvā

One day, **parva puella in silvā errabat. Puella casam videbat. Puella ianuam intrabat** without knocking. On **mensā erant** three bowls of porridge. **Puella parva occupabat magnam** bowl, **sed** she says, "This porridge **est** too **calidus!" Tunc, puella parva occupabat** medium bowl. "This porridge **est** too **frigidus!" Tunc, puella occupabat parvam** bowl. "This porridge **est bonus!"**

Puella ambulabat into the living room. Three **sellae erant** in the living room. **Sedebat in magnā sellā.** "This **sella est** too **alta." Tunc, sedebat in** medium **sellā.** "This **sella est** too **lata." Tunc, sedebat in parvā sellā.** "This **sella est bona!"**

Puella parva cubiculum intrabat. Three beds **erant in cubiculum. Puella iacebat** on **magnus** bed. "This bed **est** too **sordidus!" Tunc, puella iacebat** on the medium bed. "This bed **est** too **horrendus!" Tunc, puella** on **parva** bed **iacebat.** "This bed **est bonus!"**

Three **ursae in casā habitabat. Ursae in silvā ambulabant dum puella erat in casā. Ursae ianuam intrant. Vident** the bowls of porridge. **Spectant sellas** in the living room. **Ursae cubiculum intrant, et vident puellam parvam** in the **parvus** bed. "Hey!" **ursae clamabant.** "Help!" **puella clamabat. Puella** climbs out **fenestrā, et ursae puellam numquam vident** again.

WEEK 25: Future of Irregular Verb "Sum"

Goals: Recite "sum" in the future tense and translate.

Vocabulary

vito, vitáre, vitavi, vitatum VEE-toh, vee-TAH-ray, vee-TAH-vee, vee-TAH-toom	I avoid, to avoid, I avoided, avoided
ávarus, ávara, ávarum AH-vah-roose, AH-vah-rah, AH-vah-room	greedy
beátus, beáta, beátum bay-AH-toose, bay-AH-tah, bay-AH-toom	blessed
déxter, déxtra, déxtrum DEX-tair, DEX-trah, DEX-troom	right, right-handed
férus, féra, férum FAIR-oose, FAIR-ah, FAIR-oom	wild, fierce
fídus, fída, fídum FEE-doose, FEE-dah, FEE-doom	faithful
líber, líbera, líberum LEE-bair, LEE-bair-ah, LEE-bair-oom	free
mírus, míra, mírum MEE-roose, MEE-rah, MEE-room	strange, wonderful
réctus, récta, réctum REK-toose, REK-tah, REK-toom	straight
sánctus, sáncta, sánctum SAHNK-toose, SAHNK-tah, SAHNK-toom	holy
sínister, sínistra, sínistrum SEE-nee-stir, SEE-nee-strah, SEE-nee-stroom	left, left-handed

Chant: Future Tense Verb Sum

	Singular	English	Plural	English
1st Person	ero	I will be	erimus	we will be
2nd Person	eris	you will be	eritis	y'all will be
3rd Person	erit	he will be	erunt	they will be

Grammar Lesson

The future tense of "sum, esse, fui, futurum" is similar to the imperfect tense. We use the stem "er-" but instead of using the normal future endings, the "b" in the ending goes away when we attach it to "er-".

er-o	**er**-imus
er-is	**er**-itis
er-it	**er**-unt

The future of "sum, esse" is a **linking verb**, just like the present of that verb. It connects two Nominative nouns or adjectives together by saying that one of them *will be* the other one.

Example: Vir *erit* tabernarius.

The man *will be* a shopkeeper.

Grammar Sound Off

Review sound off from last week.

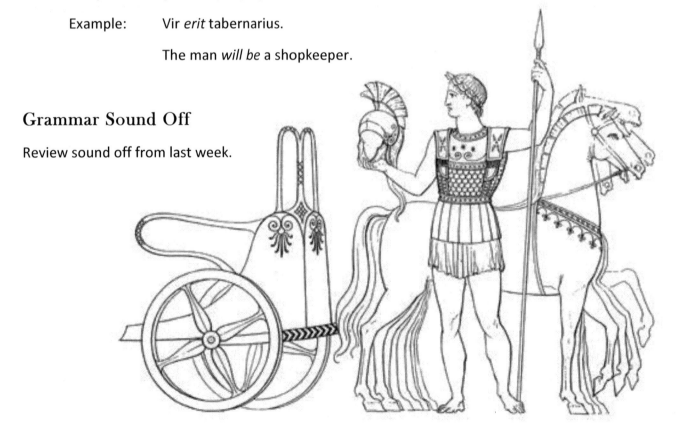

WEEK 25: Worksheet   Nomen: _____

Vocabulary: Fill in the missing parts in English and in Latin.

vito			
I avoid			

| avarus | avara | avarum | |

| beatus | | | |

| | dextra | | |

| | | ferum | |

| | | | faithful |

| liber | | | |

| | | mirum | |

| | recta | | |

| | | | holy |

| | | | left, left-handed |

Chants: Complete the chants by filling in the empty boxes.

	Present Tense of "Sum, Esse, Fui, Futurum"			
	Singular	English	Plural	English
1st Person	sum	I am		
2nd Person				
3rd Person				

	Imperfect Tense of "Sum, Esse, Fui, Futurum"			
	Singular	English	Plural	English
1st Person	eram	I was		
2nd Person				
3rd Person				

	Future Tense of "Sum, Esse, Fui, Futurum"			
	Singular	English	Plural	English
1st Person	ero	I will be		
2nd Person				
3rd Person				

Translation: Translate each verb into English. Watch the tense!

1. erimus _____
2. eras _____
3. sumus _____
4. estis _____
5. ero _____

6. erunt _____
7. erant _____
8. eram _____
9. erit _____
10. eris _____

Cases: Give just the Nominative and Accusative case endings.

	Masculine Singular	Feminine Singular	Neuter Singular	Masculine Plural	Feminine Plural	Neuter Plural
Nominative						
Accusative						

Composition: Write two sentences with the given phrase, one with the phrase as a Predicate Nominative and one as a Direct Object.

left-handed archer

PRN (Nom): Vir erit __**sinister**__ __**sagittarius**__

DO (Acc): Vir videbit __**sinistrum**__ __**sagittarium**__.

1. *greedy shopkeeper*

PRN (Nom): Germanus est _____ _____.

DO (Acc): Germanus pugnat _____ _____.

2. *holy woman*

PRN (Nom): Regina erat _____ _____.

DO (Acc): Regina vitabat _____ _____.

3. *faithful friends* (pl!)

PRN (Nom): Puellae erunt _____ _____.

DO (Acc): Puellae amabunt _____ _____.

4. *right-handed students* (pl!)

PRN (Nom): Pueri erant _____ _____.

DO (Acc): Pueri demonstrabant _____ _____.

Translation: Translate each sentence into English.

1. Eram beatus, sum gratus, et ero fidus.

2. Erimus liberi, et tunc gaudebimus.

3. Dextra femina sicam tenebat, sed sinister vir gladium tenebat.

4. Sancta via est semper recta.

5. Lupus et ursa erunt feri, sed elephantus erit mirus.

6. Avari viri erunt tabernarii in tabernā magnā.

Fabula: Read the story below. (You do not have to write anything down.)

> **Sinister Vir**
>
> Ehud **erat fidus vir** in Israel who **erat sinister, non dexter. Malus et avarus** king **oppugnabat** Israel, et **occupabat frumentum. Viri et feminae non erant liberi.**
>
> **Sanctus Deus iubebit** Ehud **pugnare malum** king. Ehud **non vitabit** his mission. Ehud **ambulabit in viā rectā** to **castellum** of the **malus** king. Ehud **narrabit feros viros** at **castellum** that **habet mirum** message for the king. **Viri feri spectabunt** Ehud. **Videbunt** that **fidus vir non habet hastam** or **gladium. Non videbunt sicam** which **sinister vir habet.**
>
> Ehud **intrabit cubiculum** where the king **erit. Narrabit** the king that **habet mirum** message from **Sanctus Deus. Tunc,** Ehud **sicam occupabit et necabit** the king. Ehud will shut **ianuas** of **cubiculum** and will run from the **castellum. Servi** of the king **verberabunt** on **ianuae, sed** the king will **non** answer **verba.** When **servi intrabunt cubiculum,** the **malus et avarus** king **erit** dead.
>
> **Viri et feminae** of Israel **erunt liberi. Gaudebunt, et erunt grati et beati.**

WEEK 26: REVIEW

Goals: Retain and recall vocabulary and grammar from weeks 22-25.

Vocabulary
Check off the ones you know.

☐	**accuso**	I accuse	☐	**horrendus**	horrendous
☐	**altus**	high, deep, tall	☐	**iaceo**	I lie down
☐	**annus**	year	☐	**iubeo**	I order
☐	**avarus**	greedy	☐	**latus**	wide
☐	**beatus**	blessed	☐	**liber**	free
☐	**calidus**	warm, hot	☐	**longus**	long
☐	**cras**	tomorrow	☐	**mirus**	strange, wonderful
☐	**creo**	I create	☐	**moneo**	I warn
☐	**dexter**	right, right-handed	☐	**multus**	much, many
☐	**doceo**	I teach	☐	**ploro**	I cry
☐	**ferus**	wild, fierce	☐	**rectus**	straight
☐	**fessus**	tired	☐	**sanctus**	holy
☐	**fidus**	faithful	☐	**sinister**	left, left-handed
☐	**frigidus**	cold	☐	**sordidus**	dirty
☐	**gaudeo**	I rejoice	☐	**specto**	I look at
☐	**gratus**	grateful	☐	**tardo**	I delay
☐	**heri**	yesterday	☐	**verbero**	I beat
☐	**hodie**	today	☐	**verbum**	word
☐	**hora**	hour	☐	**vito**	I avoid

WEEK 26: Review Worksheet

Nomen: _____

Vocabulary: Fill in the crossword puzzle with vocabulary from chapters 22-25.

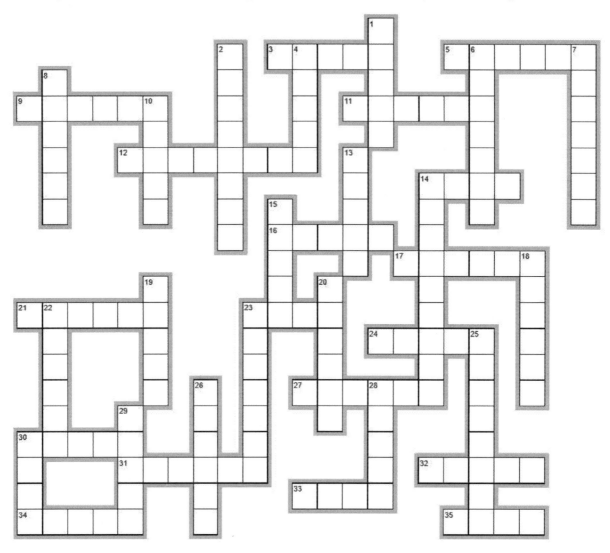

Word Bank

ACCUSO	ALTUS	ANNUS	AVARUS	BEATUS	CALIDUS	CRAS	CREO	DEXTER	DOCEO
FERUS	FESSUS	FIDUS	FRIGIDUS	GAUDEO	GRATUS	HERI	HODIE	HORA	
HORRENDUS	IACEO	IUBEO	LATUS	LIBER	LONGUS	MIRUS	MONEO	MULTUS	PLORO
RECTUS	SANCTUS	SINISTER	SORDIDUS	SPECTO	TARDO	VERBERO	VERBUM	VITO	

Across

3. I cry
5. greedy
9. word
11. right, right-handed
12. cold
14. yesterday
16. I lie down
17. grateful
21. I rejoice
23. I create
24. faithful
27. much, many
30. today
31. straight
32. high, deep, tall
33. I avoid
34. year
35. tomorrow

Down

1. I teach
2. dirty
4. wide
6. I beat
7. holy
8. tired
10. strange, wonderful
13. I order
14. horrendous
15. free
18. I look at
19. I warn
20. long
22. I accuse
23. warm, hot
25. left, left-handed
26. blessed
28. I delay
29. wild, fierce
30. hour

Chant: Fill in the blanks.

Present Tense of "gaudeo, gaudēre, gavisus sum"

	Singular	English	Plural	English
1st				
2nd				
3rd				

Imperfect Tense of "gaudeo, gaudēre, gavisus sum"

	Singular	English	Plural	English
1st				
2nd				
3rd				

Future Tense of "gaudeo, gaudēre, gavisus sum"

	Singular	English	Plural	English
1st				
2nd				
3rd				

Irregular Verb "sum, esse, fui, futurum"

	Present Tense		Imperfect Tense		Future Tense	
	Latin	*English*	*Latin*	*English*	*Latin*	*English*
1st/Sg	sum	I am	eram	I was	ero	I will be
2nd/Sg						
3rd/Sg						
1st/Pl						
2nd/Pl						
3rd/Pl						

	Verb Endings		
	Present	Imperfect	Future
1st/Sg	-o	-bam	-bo
2nd/Sg			
3rd/Sg			
1st/Pl			
2nd/Pl			
3rd/Pl			

	Verb Synopsis of "accuso, accusare, accusavi, accusatum" in the 2nd/Pl	
	Latin	*English*
Present		
Imperfect		
Future		

	Verb Synopsis of "vito, vitare, vitavi, vitatum" in the 3rd/Sg	
	Latin	*English*
Present		
Imperfect		
Future		

	First Declension Masculine EXCEPTIONS Noun/Adjective Pair	
	Singular	Plural
Nominative	agricola fidus	
Genitive		
Dative		
Accusative		
Ablative		

Noun Cases, Jobs, and Translations			
CASE	JOB	Singular	Plural
	SN, PRN	the *star*	
Dative			

Translation: Translate each sentence into Latin.

> EXAMPLE: The teachers will be faithful.
>
> ___magistr-ae___ ___erunt___ ___fidae___
> Nom/Pl/Fem   Sum → Fut/ 3ʳᵈ/Pl   Nom/Pl/Fem

1. The boys were tired.

   _____   _____   _____
   Nom/**Pl**/Masc   Sum → Imp/3ʳᵈ/**Pl**   Nom/**Pl**/Masc

2. The grateful queen will look at the words.

   _____ _____ _____ _____
   Nom/Sg/Fem   Nom/Sg /Fem   Acc/**Pl**/Neut   Verb Stem + Fut/3ʳᵈ/Sg

3. The straight river is cold and dirty.

   _____ _____ _____ _____ _____
   Nom/Sg/Masc   Nom/Sg/Masc   Sum → Pres/3ʳᵈ/Sg   Nom/Sg/Masc   Nom/Sg/Masc

4. The left-handed men will fight the wild wolves.

   _____ _____ _____ _____ _____
   Nom/**Pl**/Masc   Nom/**Pl**/Masc   Acc/**Pl**/Masc   Acc/**Pl**/Masc   V.Stem + Fut/3ʳᵈ/**Pl**

Translation: Translate each sentence into English.

1. Poeta erat servus, sed nunc est liber.

2. Agricolae iacebant, incolae sedebant, et nautae stabant.

3. Piratae feri viros sanctos iubebunt.

4. Magistra discipulos cras docebit, et beati discipuli gaudebit.

5. Verba erant bona et mira.

6. Magnos elephantos saepe spectabitis.

7. Sagittarius dexter reginam gratam monebit.

8. Multae feminae tabernarium falsum accusant.

9. Eritis boni pueri et beatae puellae.

10. Christus erat sanctus, et erimus sancti.

WEEK 27: Ablative Case: Prepositions

Goals: Memorize prepositions that go with the Ablative case and put nouns in the Ablative Singular.

Vocabulary

	máneo, manēre, mánsi, mánsum MAH-nay-oh, mah-NAY-ray, MAHN-see, MAHN-soom	I stay, to stay, I stayed, stayed
	a, ab AH, AHB	from, by, away from
	córam COR-ahm	face-to-face with
	cum COOM	with
	de DAY	down from, about
	e, ex AY, EX	from, out of
	in (+Abl.) EEN	in, on
	prae PRAY	in front of, before
	pro PRO	before, on behalf of
	síne SEE-nay	without
	sub (+Abl.) SOOB	under
	súper (+Abl.) SOO-pair	over, above, upon

Chant: First and Second Declension Endings

	Masculine Singular	Feminine Singular	Neuter Singular	Masculine Plural	Feminine Plural	Neuter Plural
Nominative	-us/-r	-a	-um	-i	-ae	-a
Genitive	-i	-ae	-i	-orum	-arum	-orum
Dative	o	-ae	o	is	is	-is
Accusative	-um	-am	-um	-os	-as	-a
Ablative	-o	a	-o	-is	-is	-is

Grammar Lesson

A **preposition** is a small word that connects a noun to the rest of the sentence. The noun that the preposition connects to the sentence is called the **object of the preposition**. In Latin, prepositions don't change endings like nouns, verbs, and adjectives. They just stay the same. But the noun that follows them changes its ending to show that it is the object of the preposition.

Some prepositions want their objects to be Ablative, and some prepositions want their objects to be Accusative. You have to memorize which case the preposition prefers! This week we have eleven prepositions that all love the **Ablative** case. You will need to put the noun following them into the Ablative case.

In your word list, you will see that a couple words have two forms: "a, ab" and "e, ex." These are like the articles "a, an" in English. You would generally use "a" or "e" before words that start with a consonant, and "ab" or "ex" before words that start with a vowel.

    ab oppido   a silvā   ex aquā   e fluvio

You will also notice three words that have (+abl.) marked after them to show they go with the Ablative. These words will show up again on a later word list where they will have a slightly different meaning when they go with the Accusative case. There are only a few prepositions that can go with either case.

Grammar Sound Off

A preposition…	…is a small word
That connects a noun…	…to the rest of the sentence.
The noun is called…	…the OP
And OP means…	…Object of the Preposition.
Some prepositions love…	…Ablative Case.
Some prepositions love…	…Accusative Case.

WEEK 27: Worksheet   Nomen: _____

Vocabulary: Fill in the missing parts in English and in Latin.

maneo			
	to stay		

	a, ab	

	coram	

	cum	

	de	

	e, ex	

	in (+abl.)	

	prae	

	pro	

	sine	

	sub (+abl.)	

	super (+abl.)	

Cases: Give just the Nominative, Accusative, and Ablative case endings.

	Masculine Singular	Feminine Singular	Neuter Singular	Masculine Plural	Feminine Plural	Neuter Plural
Nominative						
Accusative						
Ablative						

Changing Cases: Take each Nominative Singular noun and put it into the Ablative Singular case.

silva → silvā   camelus → camelo

1. tumulus → _____
2. casa → _____
3. locus → _____
4. castellum → _____
5. lupus → _____
6. cubiculum → _____
7. insula → _____
8. fluvius → _____
9. tectum → _____
10. culina → _____
11. fenestra → _____
12. murus → _____

Grammar: Fill in the blanks with info from your grammar and grammar sound-off from this week or from previous weeks.

1. A _____ is a small word that connects a _____ to the rest of the sentence.

2. The _____ the preposition connects to the sentence is called the _____ of the _____.

3. In Latin, the object of the preposition can either be in the _____ case or the _____ case.

Endings and Translation: Add the correct ending to each blank to put the word in Ablative case. Then translate the sentence.

Vir est in cas-**ā**	The man is in the house.
Puer ex oppid-**o** ambulat.	The boy walks out of the town.

1. Equi sunt pro tabern-___.

2. Poeta est coram femin-___.

3. Aqua est in fluvi-___.

4. Regina de castell-___ narrat.

5. Cibus erat sub mens-___.

6. Mensa erat prae mur-___.

7. Puer sine gladi-___ intrat.

8. Via ab oppid-___ errat.

9. Puella in insul-___ manet.

10. Nauta cum amic-___ pugnat.

Location: Circle which preposition describes the star's location in relation to the box.

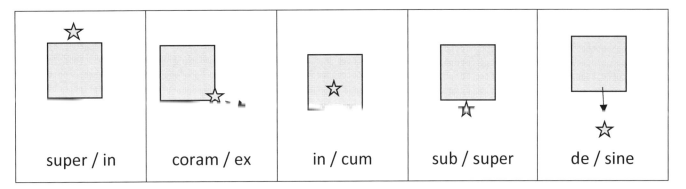

| super / in | coram / ex | in / cum | sub / super | de / sine |

Preposition Choice: Circle the preposition which makes the sentence make the most sense.

> Caelum est (**super**/ sine) terrā.
>
> 1. Campus est (**prae / cum**) castello.
> 2. Vir est (**de / coram**) feminā.
> 3. Puella ambulat (**cum / ex**) amico.
> 4. Vir ambulat (**e / coram**) casā.
> 5. Pirata narrat (**sine / de**) auro.
> 6. Poeta stat (**in / sub**) tabernā.
> 7. Vir pugnat (**e / pro**) feminā.
> 8. Nauta navigat (**a / sine**) patriā.

Fabula: Read the story below. (You do not have to write anything down.)

Fabula De Cibo

Once **erat puella** who **manebat in casā cum ursā. Puella numquam ambulabat e casā. Puella numquam videbat e fenestrā. Magnus elephantus erat prae casā, sed puella non ambulabat e casā. Aqua erat sub casā, sed puella non ambulabat e casā. Ferus lupus erat super tecto, sed puella non ambulabat e casā.** One day, a robber **casam intrabat, et cibum occupabat. Tunc,** the robber **ambulabat a casā. Irata puella spectabat** robber **e fenestra. Puella non est** able **habitare sine cibo! Puella ambulabat e casā cum ursā. Prae silvā,** the robber **erat coram puellā.** The robber **cibum non dabit** to **puella.** So, **ursa virum pugnabat pro puellā. Ursa virum verberabat, et puella cibum occupabat.** The **miser** robber **ambulabat a silvā, et puella cum ursā habebat** a picnic **e casā** for the very first time.

WEEK 28: Ablative Case: Prepositions Continued

Goal: Translate prepositional phrases with the Ablative Singular and Plural.

Vocabulary

náto, natáre, natávi, natátum NAH-toh, nah-TAH-ray, nah-TAH-vee, nah-TAH-toom	I swim, to swim, I swam, swum
vólo, voláre, volávi, volátum VOH-loh, voh-LAH-ray, voh-LAH-vee, voh-LAH-toom	I fly, to fly, I flew, flown
aquíla, aquílae (f.) ah-KWEE-lah, ah-KWEE-lay	eagle
béstia, béstiae (f.) BAY-stee-ah, BAY-stee-ay	beast
cérvus, cérvi (m.) CHAIR-voose, CHAIR-vee	deer
cétus, céti (m.) CHAY-toose, CHAY-tee	whale, sea monster
Itália, Itáliae (f.) ee-TAH-lee-ah, ee-TAH-lee-ay	Italy
oceánus, oceáni (m.) oh-chay-AH-noose, oh-chay-AH-nee	ocean
Róma, Rómae (f.) ROH-mah, ROH-may	Rome
spélunca, spéluncae (f.) SPAY-loon-cah, SPAY-loon-chay	cave
vílla, víllae (f.) VEE-lah, VEE-lay	farmhouse

Highlight Masculine nouns with blue, Feminine with pink, and Neuter with yellow.

Grammar Lesson & Sound Off

Review last week's lesson and sound off as well as the prepositions learned last week.

WEEK 28: Worksheet Nomen: _____

Vocabulary: Fill in the missing parts in English and in Latin.

nato		natavi	

	volare		
			flown

| aquila | aquilae | f. | |

| bestia | | | |

| | | | deer |

| | ceti | | |

| Italia | | | |

| | | | ocean |

| Roma | | | |

| spelunca | | | |

| | | | farmhouse |

Paideia Latina, Level A | 177

Chant: Give the Noun Cases, Jobs, and Translations

CASE	JOB	Singular	Plural
		the *eagle*	
Genitive	PNA		

Cases: Give just the Nominative, Accusative, and Ablative case endings.

	Masculine Singular	Feminine Singular	Neuter Singular	Masculine Plural	Feminine Plural	Neuter Plural
Nominative						
Accusative						
Ablative						

Changing Cases: Take each Nominative noun and put it into the Ablative case. If the Nominative is Plural, change it to Ablative Plural.

silva → silvā   silvae → silvis

1. oceanus → _____
2. oceani → _____
3. villa → _____
4. villae → _____
5. bestia → _____
6. bestiae → _____
7. castellum → _____
8. castella → _____
9. cetus → _____
10. oppida → _____
11. astrum → _____
12. cervi → _____

Word Hunt: Choose the <u>best</u> word from the box for each blank.

| nato | aquila | bestia | cervus | cetus |
| Italia | oceanus | Roma | spelunca | villa |

1. _____ is the capital city of _____.
2. The _____ is the symbol of both the United States and of Rome.
3. _____ in the swimming pool, not in the _____.
4. A blue _____ is the largest animal in the world.
5. A _____ is bigger than a *casa*.
6. "Beauty and the _____" is my favorite fairy tale.
7. A _____ has antlers and lives in a _____.

Translation: Translate each prepositional phrase from English to Latin using the correct Ablative ending.

in the ocean = in oceano

1. with the whale = _____
2. with the whales = _____
3. face-to-face with the beast = _____
4. without the beasts = _____
5. out of the farmhouse = _____
6. away from the farmhouses = _____
7. down from the hill = _____
8. about the cave = _____
9. in front of the town = _____
10. under the towns = _____

Translation: Translate each sentence into English.

1. Roma in Italiā est.

2. Cetus in oceano natat.

3. Aquila in caelo volabit.

4. Aquilae sunt super oppidis.

5. Villa erat prae tumulis.

6. Lupus est coram cervo.

7. Aquarius aquam de fluvio portabat.

8. Tabernarius de gemmis in speluncā narrabat.

Fabula: Read the story below. (You do not have to write anything down.)

Aquila et Cervus

Cervus in silvā ambulabat. Cervus ex fluvio potabat. Cervus in herbis cenebam. Cervus erat laetus et liber. Aquila in caelo volabat. Aquila super silvā erat. Tunc, aquila super campo erat. Villa erat in campo. Aquila viros videbat. Viri ab villā ambulabant et silvam intrabant. Viri sagittas habebant. Viri erant sagittarii. Viri cervum liberum oppugnabunt et necabunt. Aquila est miser. Aquila desiderat monēre cervum. Aquila volat in silvā et sedet in terrā prae fluvio. Aquila clamat et nunc cervus est coram aquilā. Aquila narrat de viris. Aquila narrat de sagittis. Cervus non stultus est. Cervus speluncam intrat et in speluncā manet. Viri cum sagittis speluncam numquam vident. Viri cum sagittis cervum numquam vident. Sed lupum vident, et desiderant necare lupum. Aquila in caelo volat. Aquila lupum non monebit. Lupus non est amicus. Cervus est amicus.

WEEK 29: Accusative Case: Prepositions

*Goals: Memorize prepositions that go with the Accusative case
and put nouns in the Accusative Singular.*

Vocabulary

festíno, festináre, festinávi, festinátum fes-TEE-noh, fes-tee-NAH-ray, fes-tee-NAH-vee, fes-tee-NAH-toom	I hurry, to hurry, I hurried, hurried
ad AHD	to, toward
ánte AHN-tay	before
ápud AH-pood	at, by, near
círcum CHUR-coom	around
cóntra CON-trah	against
éxtra EX-trah	outside of
in (+Acc.) EEN	into, onto (with motion)
ínfra EEN-frah	below
ínter EEN-tair	between, among
íntra EEN-trah	within
iúxta YOOKS-tah	near, next to

Grammar Lesson

Remember that a **preposition** is a small word that connects a noun to the rest of the sentence. The noun that the preposition connects to the sentence is called the **object of the preposition**.

Some prepositions want their objects to be Ablative, and some prepositions want their objects to be Accusative. You have to memorize which case the preposition prefers! One hint is that many of the Ablative prepositions show motion *away from* something or no motion at all, and many of the Accusative prepositions show motion *toward* something. This week we have eleven prepositions that all love the **Accusative** case. You will need to put the noun following them into the Accusative case.

Watch out especially for the preposition "in." When it is with the Ablative case, it means "in, on," but when it is with the Accusative case, it means "into, onto." The Accusative shows motion into something, but the Ablative is just showing the place in which something is.

Grammar Sound Off

A preposition...	...is a small word
That connects a noun...	...to the rest of the sentence.
The noun is called...	...the OP
And OP means...	...Object of the Preposition.
Some prepositions love...	...Ablative Case.
Motion from...	**...is Ablative Case.**
Some prepositions love...	...Accusative Case.
Motion toward...	**...is Accusative Case.**

WEEK 29: Worksheet   Nomen: _____

Vocabulary: Fill in the missing parts in English and in Latin.

festino			
		I hurried	

	ad	

	ante	

	apud	

	circum	

	contra	

	extra	

	infra	

	in (+acc.)	

	inter	

	intra	

	iuxta	

Present Tense of "festino, festinare, festinavi, festinatum"

	Singular	English	Plural	English
1st	festino	I hurry		
2nd				
3rd				

Imperfect Tense of "festino, festinare, festinavi, festinatum"

	Singular	English	Plural	English
1st	festinabam	I was hurrying		
2nd				
3rd				

Future Tense of "festino, festinare, festinavi, festinatum"

	Singular	English	Plural	English
1st	festinabo	I will hurry		
2nd				
3rd				

Cases: Give <u>all</u> case endings in all genders.

	Masculine Singular	Feminine Singular	Neuter Singular	Masculine Plural	Feminine Plural	Neuter Plural
Nominative						
Genitive						
Dative						
Accusative						
Ablative						

Changing Cases: Take each Nominative Singular noun and put it into the Accusative Singular case.

> silva → silvam   camelus → camelum
>
> 1. tumulus → _____   6. cubiculum → _____
> 2. casa → _____   7. insula → _____
> 3. locus → _____   8. fluvius → _____
> 4. castellum → _____   9. tectum → _____
> 5. oceanus → _____   10. spelunca → _____

Grammar: Fill in the blanks with info from your grammar and grammar sound-off from this week or from previous weeks.

1. The noun the preposition connects to the sentence is called the _____ of the _____.
2. In Latin, the object of the preposition can either be in the _____ case or the _____ case.
3. Frequently, prepositions in the Ablative case show motion _____.
4. Frequently, prepositions in the Accusative case show motion _____.

Preposition Choice: Circle the preposition which makes the most sense.

> Terra est (**infra** / trans) caelum.
>
> 1. Puer festinat (**ad** / **inter**) castellum.
> 2. Harena est (**ad** / **iuxta**) oceanum.
> 3. Puella ambulat (**circum** / **contra**) campum.
> 4. Forum est (**intra** / **extra**) oppidum.

Endings and Translation: Add the correct ending to each blank to put the word in Accusative case. Then translate the sentence.

| Vir est iuxta cas-**am** | The man is near the house. |
| Puer ad fluvi-**um** ambulat. | The boy walks toward the river. |

1. Ursa in spelunc-___ festinabat. _____

2. Sagittarius contra Rom-___ pugnabit. _____

3. Nauta circum ocean-___ navigat. _____

4. Silva est extra vill-___. _____

5. Castellum erat apud tumul-___. _____

6. Vir ante regin-___ stat. _____

Fabula: Read the story below. (You do not have to write anything down.)

Cetus Parvus et Oceanus Latus

Cetus parvus infra oceanum habitabat. Cetus circum oceanum numquam natabat. Parvus cetus casam in speluncā habebat. Herbae erant iuxta speluncam in aquā. Cetus in herbis cenabat. Magnae bestiae desiderabant cenare in ceto, sed cetus intra speluncam festinabat. Magnae bestiae non intrabant speluncam parvam, sed manebant extra speluncam et cetum non necabant. Nunc, cetus parvus non desiderabat manēre semper in speluncā. Desiderabat vidēre latum oceanum. Desiderabat natare circum oceanum. Cras, cetus natabit extra speluncam, inter insulas, et apud terram. Multae magnae bestiae oppugnabunt cetum, sed cetus pugnabit contra bestias et festinabit in novas speluncas. Et cetus erit laetus in lato oceano. Cetus erit liber.

WEEK 30: Accusative Case: Prepositions Continued

Goal: Translate prepositional phrases using Accusative Singular and Plural.

Vocabulary

cápto, captáre, captávi, captátum COP-toh, cop-TAH-ray, cop-TAH-vee, cop-TAH-toom	I hunt, to hunt, I hunted, hunted
ob AHB	in front of
per PAIR	through
post POHST	after
práeter PRAY-tair	past
própe PROH-pay	near
própter PROHP-tair	on account of
secúndum say-COON-doom	along, according to
sub (+ Acc.) SOOB	up to, under (with motion)
súper (+ Acc.) SOO-pair	over, above, upon (with motion)
trans TRAHNZ	across
última ULL-trah	beyond

Grammar Lesson

This week we have eleven more prepositions that all love the **Accusative** case. You will need to put the noun following them into the Accusative case.

Watch out for the prepositions "sub" and "super." Both of these prepositions can go with either the Ablative or the Accusative. When they are with the Ablative, they just show where something is. When they are with the Accusative, they show motion happening.

Aquila *super* terrā est.	The eagle is above the ground. (Ablative)
Aquila *super* terram volat.	The eagle flies over the ground. (Accusative)
Silva *sub* tumulo est.	The forest is under the hill. (Ablative)
Vir *sub* tumulum ambulat.	The man walks up to the hill. (Accusative)

Grammar Sound Off

Review last week's sound off.

WEEK 30: Worksheet　　　　　Nomen: _____

Vocabulary: Fill in the missing parts in English and in Latin.

capto			
			hunted

	ob	

	per	

	post	

	praeter	

	prope	

	propter	

	secundum	

	sub (+acc.)	

	super (+acc.)	

	trans	

	ultra	

Paideia Latina, Level A | 189

Cases: Give just the Nominative, Accusative, and Ablative case endings.

	Masculine Singular	Feminine Singular	Neuter Singular	Masculine Plural	Feminine Plural	Neuter Plural
Nominative						
Accusative						
Ablative						

Changing Cases: Take each Nominative noun and put it in the Accusative case. If the Nominative is Plural, change it to Accusative Plural.

silva → silvam   silvae → silvas

1. oceanus → _____
2. oceani → _____
3. via → _____
4. viae → _____
5. porta → _____
6. portae → _____
7. castellum → _____
8. castella → _____
9. murus → _____
10. oppida → _____
11. verbum → _____
12. horti → _____

Preposition Choice: Circle the preposition which makes the sentence make the most sense.

Castellum est (per / (ultra)) fluvium.

1. Aquila **(sub / super)** campum saepe volat.
2. Vir **(prope / per)** tumulum heri stabat.
3. Equus **(secundum / propter)** viam festinabit.
4. Vir **(per / post)** silvam ambulat.
5. Cetus **(trans / ob)** insulam natabat.

Translation: Translate each prepositional phrase from English to Latin using the correct Accusative ending.

across the ocean = trans oceanum
1. beyond the hill = _____
2. beyond the hills = _____
3. up to the farmhouse = _____
4. up to the farmhouses = _____
5. toward the gates = _____
6. on account of the gold = _____
7. along the road = _____
8. through the rivers = _____
9. toward the castle = _____
10. past the castles = _____

Translation: Translate each sentence into English.

1. Agricola et nauta ad Romam festinabant.

2. Femina tabernarium malum propter margaritas accusat.

3. Magistra prope mensam stat, et discipuli ob sellas stant.

4. Ante bellum, viri cervos feros captabunt.

5. Discipuli secundum viam et praeter casas ambulant.

Preposition Sort: Draw a line from the preposition to the Accusative Case or the Ablative case to show which case it loves. Some may have more than one case.

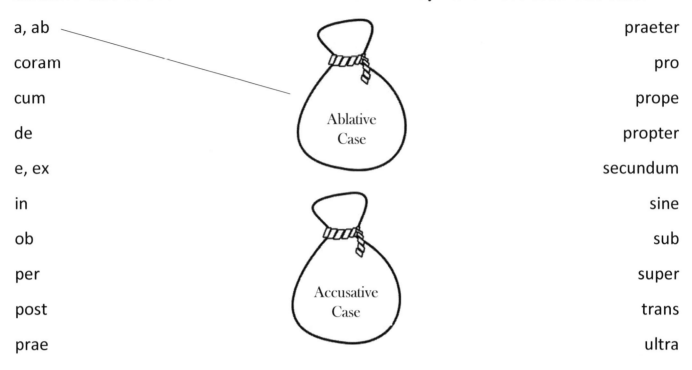

a, ab		praeter
coram		pro
cum		prope
de		propter
e, ex		secundum
in		sine
ob		sub
per		super
post		trans
prae		ultra

Fabula: Read the story below. (You do not have to write anything down.)

Piratae Contra Nautas

Piratae mali intra castellum in insulā habitabant. Multi nautae trans oceanum ad insulam navigabant propter aurum. Nautae piratas captare et oppugnare et necare desiderant. Nautae avari aurum in insulā desiderant. Sed piratae sunt feri, et non dabunt aurum. Ante bellum, nautae secundum harenam navigabant. Spectabant silvam in insulā. Per silvam erat tumulus. Super tumulo erat castellum. Nautae ex aquā et trans harenam festinant. Praeter silvam et sub tumulum festinant. Piratae viros prae castello vident. Piratae clamant! Piratae de castello festinant et nautas oppugnant. Bellum est ferum! Piratae sunt coram nautis. Gladii scuta verberant. Sagittae in caelo volant.

Tunc, sanctus vir ambulat ex speluncā prope castellum. Sanctus vir inter piratas et nautas stat. "Piratae sunt mali!" sanctus vir narrat. "Sed nautae sunt avari! Amatis aurum. Non amatis insulam. Non amatis viros et feminas. Non amatis Deum." Verba sunt bona. Piratae plorant. Nautae plorant. Post bellum, nautae trans oceanum navigant, et piratae ultra insulam navigant sine auro. Sed sanctus vir in insulā intra speluncam manet, et aurum in insulā intra castellum manet.

WEEK 31: REVIEW

Goals: Retain and recall vocabulary and grammar from weeks 27-30.

Vocabulary

Check off the ones you know.

☐	a, ab	from, by, away from	☐	maneo	I stay
☐	ad	to, toward	☐	nato	I swim
☐	ante	before	☐	ob	in front of
☐	apud	at, by, near	☐	oceanus	ocean
☐	aquila	eagle	☐	per	through
☐	bestia	beast	☐	post	after
☐	capto	I hunt	☐	prae	in front of, before
☐	cervus	deer	☐	praeter	past
☐	cetus	whale, sea monster	☐	pro	before, on behalf of
☐	circum	around	☐	prope	near
☐	contra	against	☐	propter	on account of
☐	coram	face-to-face with	☐	Roma	Rome
☐	cum	with	☐	secundum	along
☐	de	down from, about	☐	sine	without
☐	e, ex	from, out of	☐	spelunca	cave
☐	extra	outside of	☐	sub (+abl.)	under
☐	festino	I hurry	☐	sub (+acc.)	up to, under
☐	in (+abl.)	in, on	☐	super (+abl.)	over, above, upon
☐	in (+acc.)	into, onto	☐	super (+acc.)	over, above, upon
☐	infra	below	☐	trans	across
☐	inter	between, among	☐	ultra	beyond
☐	intra	within	☐	villa	farmhouse
☐	Italia	Italy	☐	volo	I fly
☐	iuxta	near, next to			

WEEK 31: Review Worksheet   Nomen: _____

Vocabulary: Fill in the crossword puzzle with vocabulary from chapters 27-30.

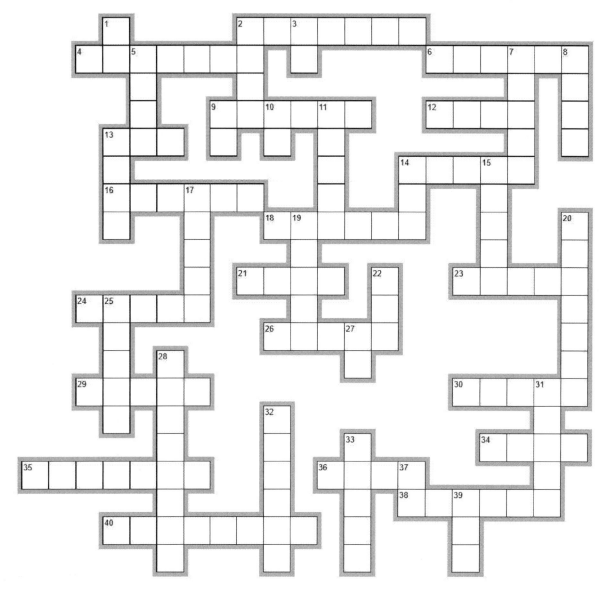

Word Bank

AB	AD	ANTE	APUD	AQUILA	BESTIA	CAPTO	CERVUS	CETUS	CIRCUM	CONTRA
CORAM	CUM	DE	EX	EXTRA	FESTINO	IN	INFRA	INTER	INTRA	ITALIA	IUXTA
MANEO	NATO	OB	OCEANUS	PER	POST	PRAE	PRAETER	PRO	PROPE	PROPTER
ROMA	SECUNDUM	SINE	SPELUNCA	SUB	SUPER	TRANS	ULTRA	VILLA	VOLO

194 | Paideia Latina, Level A

Across

2. past
4. I hurry
6. against
9. Italy
12. Rome
13. through
14. whale, sea monster
16. eagle
18. around
21. before
23. I hunt
24. farmhouse
26. I stay
29. near
30. over, above, upon (abl, acc)
34. I swim
35. ocean
36. I fly
38. beast
40. along

Down

1. down from, about
2. after
3. to, toward
5. without
7. across
8. at, by, near
9. in, on (abl); into, onto (acc.)
10. from, by, away from
11. between, among
13. in front of, before
14. with
15. beyond
17. near, next to
19. within
20. on account of
22. before, on behalf of
25. below
27. from, out of
28. cave
31. outside of
32. deer
33. face-to-face with
37. in front of
39. under (abl); under, up to (acc)

Cases: Give all case endings in all genders.

	Masculine Singular	Feminine Singular	Neuter Singular	Masculine Plural	Feminine Plural	Neuter Plural
Nominative						
Genitive						
Dative						
Accusative						
Ablative						

Translation: Circle whether the preposition wants Ablative or Accusative and then translate the phrase into Latin using the correct case ending.

	across the river	(Abl /(Acc))	trans fluvium
1.	in the water	(Abl / Acc)	_____
2.	into the water	(Abl / Acc)	_____
3.	beyond the garden	(Abl / Acc)	_____
4.	outside of the house	(Abl / Acc)	_____
5.	outside of the houses	(Abl / Acc)	_____
6.	in front of the forest	(Abl / Acc)	_____
7.	with the friend	(Abl / Acc)	_____
8.	with the friends	(Abl / Acc)	_____
9.	above the ground	(Abl / Acc)	_____
10.	along the road	(Abl / Acc)	_____
11.	between the towns	(Abl / Acc)	_____
12.	before the war	(Abl / Acc)	_____
13.	toward the castle	(Abl / Acc)	_____
14.	away from the castles	(Abl / Acc)	_____
15.	near the moon	(Abl / Acc)	_____

Translation: Translate the sentences into English.

1. Sagittarius fidus ad castellum festinat.

2. Germana grata est intra villam.

3. Sanctus vir prae templo orat.

4. Aedificium erat inter silvam et fluvium.

5. Aquila parva super tumulum volabat, et cetus magnus trans oceanum natabat.

6. Tabernarius dubius ex oppido sordido sine amicis ambulabat.

7. Viri cervum extra speluncam captabunt.

8. Nautae avari contra piratas malos in insulā pugnant.

9. Puer ab insulā natabat, et erat coram ceto.

10. Aquarius propter aquam ultra oppidum ambulat.

11. Femina prope villam manet, sed agricola in agris laborat.

WEEKS 32 & 33: CUMULATIVE REVIEW

Goals: Retain and recall vocabulary, chants, and grammar from entire book.

Vocabulary

Review the vocabulary from the chapters or from the glossary at the back of the book. Drill yourself or drill with another student. Make notes which words you need to study.

Chants

Review the chants from the chapters or from the reference pages at the back of the book. Chant the endings aloud. Chant the endings attached to words. Make notes which ones you need to study.

Grammar Sound Offs

Review the grammar sound offs from each lesson. Cover up the right hand side of the chant and see if you know what to say.

WEEK 32: Cumulative Review Worksheet   Nomen: _____

Chants: Fill in the empty blanks.

	First and Second Declension Noun/Adjective Endings					
	Masculine Singular	Feminine Singular	Neuter Singular	Masculine Plural	Feminine Plural	Neuter Plural
Nominative	-us/-r	-a	-um			
Genitive						
Dative						
Accusative						
Ablative						

1. What is the Nom/Pl/Masc ending? _____
2. What is the Acc/Sg/Fem ending? _____
3. What is the Abl/Pl/Neut ending? _____
4. What is the Abl/Sg/Fem ending? _____
5. What is the Acc/Sg/Masc ending? _____

Chant: Cases, Jobs, and Translations			
CASE	JOB	Singular	Plural
Nominative		the *noun*	
	IO		

Paideia Latina, Level A | 199

Verb Stems: Find the verb stem of each verb.

    capto, captare, captavi, captatum → capta-

1. rogo, rogare, rogavi, rogatum → _____
2. maneo, manēre, mansi mansum → _____
3. do, dare, dedi, datum → _____
4. volo, volare, volavi, volatum → _____
5. sedeo, sedēre, sedi, sessum → _____

Chants: Fill in the empty blanks.

	Present Tense of "do, dare, dedi, datum"			
	Singular	English	Plural	English
1st Person	do	I give		
2nd Person				
3rd Person				

	Imperfect Tense of "do, dare, dedi, datum"			
	Singular	English	Plural	English
1st Person				
2nd Person				
3rd Person				

	Future Tense of "do, dare, dedi, datum"			
	Singular	English	Plural	English
1st Person				
2nd Person				
3rd Person				

Translation: Translate these sentences from English to Latin.

1. My brother works near the town.

   _____   _____   _____   _____   _____
   Nom/Sg/Masc   Nom/Sg/Masc   Prep   Acc/Sg/Neut   V. Stem + Pres/3rd/Sg

2. The beautiful queen will rejoice on account of the horses.

   _____   _____   _____   _____   _____
   Nom/Sg/Fem   Nom/Sg/Fem   Prep   Acc/**Pl**/Masc   V. Stem + Fut/3rd/Sg

3. The foolish settlers were hastening away from the cave.

   _____   _____   _____   _____   _____
   Nom/**Pl**/Masc   Nom/**Pl**/Masc   Prep   Abl/Sg/Fem   V. Stem + Imp/3rd/**Pl**

4. Your daughter tells stories about a wolf.

   _____   _____   _____   ____   _____   _____
   Nom/Sg/Fem   Nom/Sg/Fem   Acc/**Pl**/Fem   Prep   Abl/Sg/Masc   V. Stem + Pres/3rd/Sg

5. The female servants wander into the forest on the island.

   _____   ____   _____   ____   _____   _____
   Nom/**Pl**/Fem   Prep   Acc/Sg/Fem   Prep   Abl/Sg/Fem   V. Stem + Pres/3rd/**Pl**

6. The shopkeeper was desiring gold, silver, and gems.

   _____   _____   _____   ____   _____   _____
   Nom/Sg/Masc   Acc/Sg/Neut   Acc/Sg/Neut   Acc/**Pl**/Fem   V. Stem + Imp/3rd/Sg

7. We will pray in front of the large temple.

   ____   _____   _____   _____
   Prep   Acc/Sg/Neut *or*   Acc/Sg/Neut *or*   V. Stem + Fut/1st/**Pl**

   Abl/Sg/Neut   Abl/Sg/Neut

Translation: Translate these sentences into English.

1. Hodie, filia mensam parat, et ex culinā cibum portat.

2. Camelus elephantum apud fluvium videbat, et ambulabat trans campum.

3. Ventus per rosas in horto flat dum aquila super tumulum volat.

4. Viri scuta et gladios occupabant, et pro Romā pugnabant.

5. Harena est calida, sed aqua est frigida.

6. Magister in Italiā habitabat, et multos discipulos docebat.

7. Christus est verus Deus, et terram et caelum creabat.

8. Accusabatis avaram feminam, et femina plorabat.

9. Equus viam rectam vitabit, et vir equum malum verberabit.

WEEK 33: Cumulative Review Worksheet   Nomen: _____

Chants: Fill in the blanks.

	Irregular Verb "sum, esse, fui, futurum"					
	Present Tense		Imperfect Tense		Future Tense	
	Latin	English	Latin	English	Latin	English
1st/Sg	sum	I am	eram	I was	ero	I will be
2nd/Sg						
3rd/Sg						
1st/Pl						
2nd/Pl						
3rd/Pl						

	Verb Endings		
	Present	Imperfect	Future
1st/Sg	-o	-bam	-bo
2nd/Sg			
3rd/Sg			
1st/Pl			
2nd/Pl			
3rd/Pl			

	Verb Synopsis of "amo, amare, amavi, amatum" in the 2nd/Pl	
	Latin	English
Present		
Imperfect		
Future		

	Verb Synopsis of "iaceo, iacēre, iacui, ---" in the 3rd/Pl	
	Latin	English
Present		
Imperfect		
Future		

	Verb Synopsis of "nato, natare, navi, natatum" in the 3rd/Sg	
	Latin	English
Present		
Imperfect		
Future		

	Masculine Singular	Feminine Singular	Neuter Singular	Masculine Plural	Feminine Plural	Neuter Plural
Nominative						
Accusative						
Ablative						

Case Swap: Change each Nominative to to Accusative and then to Ablative. If the Nominative is Plural, keep it Plural in the new case.

Nominative		Accusative		Ablative
cubiculum	→	cubiculum	→	cubiculo
1. rosa	→	_____	→	_____
2. stilus	→	_____	→	_____
3. vinum	→	_____	→	_____
4. vina	→	_____	→	_____
5. horae	→	_____	→	_____
6. anni	→	_____	→	_____

Translation: Translate these sentences from English to Latin.

1. The dear sister looks at the moon.

   _____ _____ _____ _____
   Nom/Sg/Fem Nom/Sg/Fem Acc/Sg/Fem Verb Stem + Pres/3rd/Sg

2. The pirates were ugly and fierce.

   _____ _____ _____ __ _____
   Nom/Pl/Masc* Sum → Imp/3rd/Pl Nom/Pl/Masc   Nom/Pl/Masc

3. The archer will be sad and angry.

   _____ _____ _____ __ _____
   Nom/Sg/Masc Sum → Fut/3rd/Sg Nom/Sg/Masc   Nom/Sg/Masc

4. We love God, and we are free and faithful.

   _____ _____ __ _____ _____ __ _____
   Acc/Sg/Masc V. Stem + Pres/1st/Pl   Sum → Pres/1st/Pl Nom/Pl/Masc   Nom/Pl/Masc

5. The wine is good, and the town is happy.

   _____ _____ _____ __ _____ _____ _____
   Nom/Sg/Neut Sum→Pres/3rd/Sg Nom/Sg/Neut   Nom/Sg/Neut Sum→Pres/3rd/Sg Nom/Sg/Neut

6. After many hours, the teacher will praise the students.

   _____ _____ _____ _____ _____ _____
   Prep Acc/Pl/Fem Acc/Pl/Fem Nom/Sg/Masc Acc/Pl/Masc V. Stem + Fut/3rd/Sg

7. The man was sitting within the whale.

   _____ _____ _____ _____
   Nom/Sg/Masc Prep Acc/Sg/Masc V. Stem + Imp/3rd/Sg

Translation: Translate these sentences into English.

1. Heri, cervus aquam e fluvio potabat.

2. Scriba dominum malum iuvat, et frumentum ab agricolis occupat.

3. Femina iuxta fenestram puerum parvum extra casam vocabat.

4. Poeta paratus verba vera nunc cantabit.

5. Germani erant magni, sed germanae erant parvae.

6. Insula in oceano est, et multam silvam habet.

7. Fabula tua erit falsa, et verba tua erunt dubia.

8. Magistra bona mensas apud ludum ornabat.

9. Sagittarius galeam demonstrat et sagittas tenet.

REFERENCE PAGES: CHANTS AND GLOSSARY

Chant: First and Second Declension Noun/Adjective Endings

	Masculine Singular	Feminine Singular	Neuter Singular	Masculine Plural	Feminine Plural	Neuter Plural
Nominative	-us/-r	-a	-um	-i	-ae	-a
Genitive	-i	-ae	-i	-orum	-arum	-orum
Dative	-o	-ae	-o	-is	-is	-is
Accusative	-um	-am	-um	-os	-as	-a
Ablative	-o	a	-o	-is	-is	-is

Chant: Cases, Jobs, and Translations

CASE	JOB	Singular	Plural
Nominative	SN, PRN	the *noun*	the *nouns*
Genitive	PNA	of the *noun*, the *noun's*	of the *nouns*, the *nouns'*
Dative	IO	to/for the *noun*	to/for the *nouns*
Accusative	DO, OP	the *noun*	the *nouns*
Ablative	OP	by/with/from the *noun*	by/with/from the *nouns*

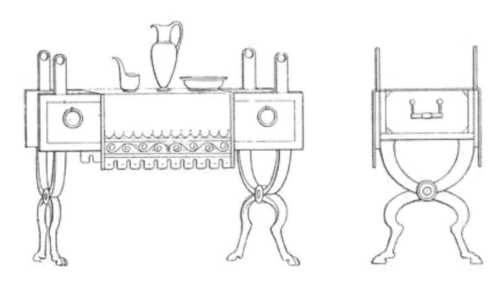

Chant: Present Tense Verb Endings

	Singular	Plural
1st Person	-o	-mus
2nd Person	-s	-tis
3rd Person	-t	-nt

Chant: Present Tense Verb Amo

	Singular	English	Plural	English
1st Person	amo	I love	amamus	we love
2nd Person	amas	you love	amatis	y'all love
3rd Person	amat	he/she/it loves	amant	they love

Chant: Present Tense Verb Video

	Singular	English	Plural	English
1st Person	video	I see	videmus	we see
2nd Person	vides	you see	videtis	y'all see
3rd Person	videt	he/she/it sees	vident	they see

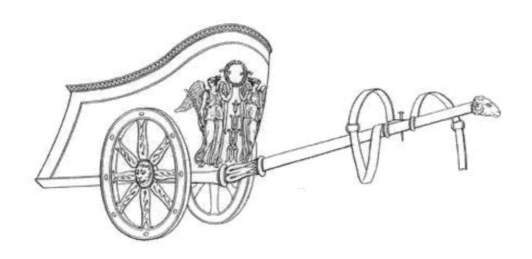

Chant: Imperfect Tense Verb Endings

	Singular	Plural
1st Person	-bam	-bamus
2nd Person	-bas	-batis
3rd Person	-bat	-bant

Chant: Imperfect Tense Verb Amo

	Singular	English	Plural	English
1st	amabam	I was loving	amabamus	we were loving
2nd	amabas	you were loving	amabatis	y'all were loving
3rd	amabat	he was loving	amabant	they were loving

Chant: Imperfect Tense Verb Video

	Singular	English	Plural	English
1st	videbam	I was seeing	videbamus	we were seeing
2nd	videbas	you were seeing	videbatis	y'all were seeing
3rd	videbat	he was seeing	videbant	they were seeing

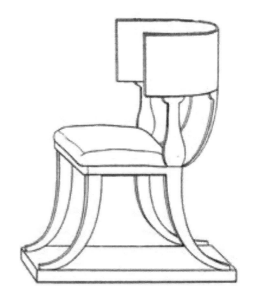

Chant: Future Tense Verb Endings

	Singular	Plural
1st Person	-bo	-bimus
2nd Person	-bis	-bitis
3rd Person	-bit	-bunt

Chant: Future Tense Verb Amo

	Singular	English	Plural	English
1st	amabo	I will love	amabimus	we will love
2nd	amabis	you will love	amabitis	y'all will love
3rd	amabit	he will love	amabunt	they will love

Chant: Future Tense Verb Video

	Singular	English	Plural	English
1st	videbo	I will see	videbimus	we will see
2nd	videbis	you will see	videbitis	y'all will see
3rd	videbit	he will see	videbunt	they will see

Chant: Present, Imperfect, Future Verb Endings

	Present	Imperfect	Future
1st/Sg	-o	-bam	-bo
2nd/Sg	-s	-bas	-bis
3rd/Sg	-t	-bat	-bit
1st/Pl	-mus	-bamus	-bimus
2nd/Pl	-tis	-batis	-bitis
3rd/Pl	-nt	-bant	-bunt

Chant: Present Tense Verb Sum

	Singular	English	Plural	English
1st Person	sum	I am	sumus	we are
2nd Person	es	you are	estis	you all are
3rd Person	est	he/she/it is	sunt	they are

Chant: Imperfect Tense Verb Sum

	Singular	English	Plural	English
1st Person	eram	I was	eramus	we were
2nd Person	eras	you were	eratis	y'all were
3rd Person	erat	he/she/it was	erant	they were

Chant: Future Tense Verb Sum

	Singular	English	Plural	English
1st Person	ero	I will be	erimus	we will be
2nd Person	eris	you will be	eritis	y'all will be
3rd Person	erit	he will be	erunt	they will be

Latin-to-English Glossary

A	a, ab (+abl.)	from, by, away from
	accuso, accusare, accusavi, accusatum	I accuse, to accuse, I accused, accused
	ad (+acc.)	to, toward
	aedificium, aedificii (n.)	building
	aedifico, aedificare, aedificavi, aedificatum	I build, to build, I built, built
	ager, agri (m.)	field (for farming)
	agricola, agricolae (m.)	farmer
	altus, alta, altum	high, deep, tall
	ambulo, ambulare, ambulavi, ambulatum	I walk, to walk, I walked, walked
	amica, amicae (f.)	female friend
	amicus, amici (m.)	male friend
	amo, amare, amavi, amatum	I love, to love, I loved, loved
	annus, anni (m.)	year
	ante (+acc.)	before
	antiquus, antiqua, antiquum	old
	aptus, apta, aptum	fitting, suitable
	apud (+acc.)	at, by, near
	aqua, aquae (f.)	water
	aquarius, aquarii (m.)	water-carrier
	aquila, aquilae (f.)	eagle
	argentum, argenti (n.)	silver
	aro, arare, aravi, aratum	I plow, to plow, I plowed, plowed
	astrum, astri (n.)	star
	auriga, aurigae (m.)	charioteer
	aurum, auri (n.)	gold
	avarus, avara, avarum	greedy
B	beatus, beata, beatum	blessed
	bellum, belli (n.)	war
	bestia, bestiae (f.)	beast
	bonus, bona, bonum	good
C	caelum, caeli (n.)	sky, heaven
	calidus, calida, calidum	warm, hot
	camelus, cameli (m.)	camel
	campus, campi (m.)	plain, field
	canto, cantare, cantavi, cantatum	I sing, to sing, I sang, sung
	capto, captare, captavi, captatum	I hunt, to hunt, I hunted, hunted
	carus, cara, carum	dear
	casa, casae (f.)	house

castellum, castelli (n.)	castle, fortress
cena, cenae (f.)	dinner
ceno, cenare, cenavi, cenatum	I dine, to dine, I dined, dined
cervus, cervi (m.)	deer
cetus, ceti (m.)	whale, sea monster
Christus, Christi (m.)	Christ
cibus, cibi (m.)	food
circum (+acc.)	around
clamo, clamare, clamavi, clamatum	I shout, to shout, I shouted, shouted
contra (+acc.)	against
coram (+abl.)	face-to-face with
cras	tomorrow
creo, creare, creavi, creatum	I create, to create, I created, created
cubiculum, cubiculi (n.)	bedroom
culina, culinae	kitchen
cum (+abl.)	with

D

de (+abl.)	down from, about
demonstro, demonstrare, demonstravi, demonstratum	I point out, to point out, I pointed out, pointed out
desidero, desiderare, desideravi, desideratum	I desire, to desire, I desired, desired
deus, dei (m.)	god
dexter, dextra, dextrum	right, right-handed
discipula, discipulae (f.)	female student
discipulus, discipuli (m.)	male student
do, dare, dedi, datum	I give, to give, I gave, given
doceo, docere, docui, doctum	I teach, to teach, I taught, taught
dominus, domini (m.)	lord, master
donum, doni (n.)	gift
dubius, -a, -um	doubtful
dum	while

E

e, ex (+abl.)	from, out of
elephantus, elephanti (m.)	elephant
equus, equi (m.)	horse
erro, errare, erravi, erratum	I wander, to wander, I wandered, wandered
et	and
extra (+acc.)	outside of

F

fabula, fabulae (f.)	story
falsus, falsa, falsum	false
femina, feminae (f.)	woman
fenestra, fenestrae	window
ferus, fera, ferum	wild, fierce
fessus, fessa, fessum	tired

	festino, festinare, festinavi, festinatum	I hurry, to hurry, I hurried, hurried
	fidus, fida, fidum	faithful
	filia, filiae (f.)	daughter
	filius, filii (m.)	son
	flo, flare, flavi, flatum	I blow, to blow, I blew, blown
	fluvius, fluvii (m.)	river
	foedus, foeda, foedum	ugly
	forum, fori (n.)	marketplace
	frigidus, frigida, frigidum	cold
	frumentum, frumenti (n.)	grain
	galea, galeae (f.)	helmet
G	gaudeo, gaudere, gavisus sum, ---	I rejoice, to rejoice, I rejoiced, ---
	gemma, gemmae (f.)	gem
	germana, germanae (f.)	sister
	germanus, germani (m.)	brother
	gladius, gladii (m.)	sword
	gratus, grata, gratum	grateful
	habeo, habēre, habui, habitum	I have, to have, I had, had
H	habito, habitare, habitavi, habitatum	I live, to live, I lived, lived
	harena, harenae (f.)	sand
	hasta, hastae (f.)	spear
	herba, herbae (f.)	herb, grass, plant
	heri	yesterday
	hodie	today
	hora, horae (f.)	hour
	horrendus, horrenda, horrendum	horrendous
	hortus, horti (m.)	garden
	iaceo, iacere, iacui, ---	I lie down, to lie down, I lay down, ---
I	ianua, -ae (f.)	door
	in (+abl.)	in, on
	in (+acc.)	into, onto
	incola, incolae (m.)	settler
	infra (+acc.)	below
	insula, insulae (f.)	island
	inter (+acc.)	between, among
	intra (+acc.)	within
	intro, intrare, intravi, intratum	I enter, to enter, I entered, entered
	ira, irae (f.)	anger
	iratus, irata, iratum	angry
	Italia, Italiae (f.)	Italy
	iubeo, iubēre, iussi, iussum	I order, to order, I ordered, ordered
	iuvo, iuvare, iuvi, iutum	I help, to help, I helped, helped
	iuxta (+acc.)	near, next to

L

laboro, laborare, laboravi, laboratum	I work, to work, I worked, worked
laetus, laeta, laetum	happy
latus, lata, latum	wide
laudo, laudare, laudavi, laudatum	I praise, to praise, I praised, praised
liber, libera, liberum	free
linea, lineae (f.)	line, string
locus, loci (m.)	place
longus, longa, longum	long
ludus, ludi (m.)	school, game
luna, lunae (f.)	moon
lupus, lupi (m.)	wolf

M

magister, magistri (m.)	male teacher
magistra, magistrae (f.)	female teacher
magnus, magna, magnum	large, great
malus, mala, malum	bad, evil
maneo, manēre, mansi, mansum	I stay, to stay, I stayed, stayed
margarita, margaritae (f.)	pearl
mensa, mensae (f.)	table
meus, mea, meum	my, mine
mirus, mira, mirum	strange, wonderful
miser, misera, miserum	sad, wretched
moneo, monēre, monui, monitum	I warn, to warn, I warned, warned
moveo, movēre, movi, motum	I move, to move, I moved, moved
multus, multa, multum	much (sg.), many (pl.)
murus, muri (m.)	wall

N

narro, narrare, narravi, narratum	I tell, to tell, I told, told
nato, natare, natavi, natatum	I swim, to swim, I swam, swum
nauta, nautae (m.)	sailor
navigo, navigare, navigavi, navigatum	I sail, to sail, I sailed, sailed
neco, necare, necavi, necatum	I kill, to kill, I killed, killed
non	not
novus, nova, novum	new
numquam	never
nunc	now

O

ob (+acc.)	in front of
occupo, occupare, occupavi, occupatum	I seize, to seize, I seized, seized
oceanus, oceani (m.)	ocean
oppidum, oppidi (n.)	town
oppugno, oppugnare, oppugnavi, oppugnatum	I attack, to attack, I attacked, attacked
orno, ornare, ornavi, ornatum	I decorate, to decorate, I decorated, decorated
oro, orare, oravi, oratum	I pray, to pray, I prayed, prayed

P

pagina, paginae (f.)	page
paratus, parata, paratum	prepared
paro, parare, paravi, paratum	I prepare, to prepare, I prepared, prepared
parvus, parva, parvum	small, little
patria, patriae (f.)	fatherland, country
per (+acc.)	through
pirata, piratae (m.)	pirate
ploro, plorare, ploravi, ploratum	I cry, to cry, I cried, cried
poeta, poetae (m.)	poet
porta, portae (f.)	gate
porto, portare, portavi, portatum	I carry, to carry, I carried, carried
post (+acc.)	after
poto, potare, potavi, potatum	I drink, to drink, I drank, drunk
prae (+abl.)	in front of, before
praeter (+acc.)	past
pro (+abl.)	before, on behalf of
prope (+acc.)	near
propter (+acc.)	on account of
puella, puellae (f.)	girl
puer, pueri (m.)	boy
pugno, pugnare, pugnavi, pugnatum	I fight, to fight, I fought, fought
pulcher, pulchra, pulchrum	beautiful, handsome

R

rectus, recta, rectum	straight
regina, reginae (f.)	queen
rogo, rogare, rogavi, rogatum	I ask, to ask, I asked, asked
Roma, Romae (f.)	Rome
rosa, rosae (f.)	rose

S

saepe	often
sagitta, sagittae (f.)	arrow
sagittarius, sagittarii (m.)	archer
sanctus, sancta, sanctum	holy
scriba, scribae (m.)	scribe
scutum, scuti (n.)	shield
secundum (+acc.)	along, according to
sed	but
sedeo, sedēre, sedi, sessum	I sit, to sit, I sat, sat
sella, sellae (f.)	chair
semper	always
serva, servae (f.)	female slave, female servant
servus, servi (m.)	male slave, male servant
sica, sicae (f.)	dagger
silva, silvae (f.)	forest, woods
sine (+abl.)	without

sinister, sinistra, sinistrum	left, left-handed
sordidus, sordida, sordidum	dirty
specto, spectare, spectavi, spectatum	I look at, to look at, I looked at, seen
spelunca, speluncae (f.)	cave
stella, stellae (f.)	star
stilus, stili (m.)	stylus, pen
sto, stare, steti, statum	I stand, to stand, I stood, stood
stultus, stulta, stultum	foolish
sub (+abl)	under
sub (+acc.)	under, up to
sum, esse, fui, futurum	I am, to be, I was, about to be
super (+abl. or +acc.)	over, above, upon
taberna, tabernae (f.)	shop
tabernarius, tabernarii	shopkeeper
tardo, tardare, tardavi, tardatum	I delay, to delay, I delayed, delayed
tectum, tecti (n.)	roof
templum, templi (n.)	temple
teneo, tenēre, tenui, tentum	I hold, to hold, I held, held
terra, terrae (f.)	earth, ground, land
trans (+acc.)	across
tumulus, tumuli (m.)	hill
tunc	then
tuus, tua, tuum	your, yours
ultra (+acc.)	beyond
ursa, ursae (f.)	bear
ventus, venti (m.)	wind
verbero, verberare, verberavi, verberatum	I beat, to beat, I beat, beaten
verbum, verbi (n.)	word
verus, vera, verum	true
via, viae (f.)	road, way, street
victoria, victoriae (f.)	victory
video, vidēre, vidi, visum	I see, to see, I saw, seen
villa, villae (f.)	farmhouse
vinum, vini (n.)	wine
vir, viri (m.)	man
vito, vitare, vitavi, vitatum	I avoid, to avoid, I avoided, avoided
voco, vocare, vocavi, vocatum	I call, to call, I called, called
volo, volare, volavi, volatum	I fly, to fly, I flew, flown

English-to-Latin Glossary

A

about	de (+abl.)
above	super (+abl. or +acc.)
according to	secundum (+acc.)
accuse (verb)	accuso, accusare, accusavi, accusatum
across	trans (+acc.)
after	post (+acc.)
against	contra (+acc.)
along	secundum (+acc.)
always	semper
among	inter (+acc.)
and	et
anger	ira, irae (f.)
angry	iratus, irata, iratum
archer	sagittarius, sagittarii (m.)
around	circum (+acc.)
arrow	sagitta, sagittae (f.)
ask (verb)	rogo, rogare, rogavi, rogatum
at	apud (+acc.)
attack (verb)	oppugno, oppugnare, oppugnavi, oppugnatum
avoid (verb)	vito, vitare, vitavi, vitatum
away from	a/ab (+abl.)

B

bad	malus, mala, malum
bear (animal)	ursa, ursae (f.)
beast	bestia, bestiae (f.)
beat (verb)	verbero, verberare, verberavi, verberatum
beautiful	pulcher, pulchra, pulchrum
bedroom	cubiculum, cubiculi (n.)
before	ante (+acc.); prae (+abl.); pro (+abl.)
below	infra (+acc.)
between	inter (+acc.)
beyond	ultra (+acc.)
blessed	beatus, beata, beatum
blow (verb)	flo, flare, flavi, flatum
boy	puer, pueri (m.)
brother	germanus, germani (m.)
build (verb)	aedifico, aedificare, aedificavi, aedificatum
building	aedificium, aedificii (n.)
but	sed
by	a, ab (+abl.); apud (+acc.)

C

call (verb)	voco, vocare, vocavi, vocatum
camel	camelus, cameli (m.)
carry (verb)	porto, portare, portavi, portatum
castle	castellum, castelli (n.)
cave	spelunca, speluncae (f.)
chair	sella, sellae (f.)
charioteer	auriga, aurigae (m.)
Christ	Christus, Christi (m.)
cold	frigidus, frigida, frigidum
country	patria, patriae (f.)
create (verb)	creo, creare, creavi, creatum
cry (verb)	ploro, plorare, ploravi, ploratum

D

dagger	sica, sicae (f.)
daughter	filia, filiae (f.)
dear	carus, cara, carum
decorate (verb)	orno, ornare, ornavi, ornatum
deep	altus, alta, altum
deer	cervus, cervi (m.)
delay (verb)	tardo, tardare, tardavi, tardatum
desire (verb)	desidero, desiderare, desideravi, desideratum
dine (verb)	ceno, cenare, cenavi, cenatum
dinner	cena, cenae (f.)
dirty	sordidus, -a, -um

door	ianua, -ae (f.)
doubtful	dubius, -a, -um
down from	de (+abl.)
drink (verb)	poto, potare, potavi, potatum

E

eagle	aquila, aquilae (f.)
earth	terra, terrae (f.)
elephant	elephantus, elephanti (m.)
enter (verb)	intro, intrare, intravi, intratum
evil	malus, mala, malum

F

face-to-face with	coram (+abl.)
faithful	fidus, fida, fidum
false	falsus, falsa, falsum
farmer	agricola, agricolae (m.)
farmhouse	villa, villae (f.)
fatherland	patria, patriae (f.)
field (for farming)	ager, agri (m.)
field (level space)	campus, campi (m.)
fierce	ferus, fera, ferum
fight (verb)	pugno, pugnare, pugnavi, pugnatum
fitting	aptus, apta, aptum
fly (verb)	volo, volare, volavi, volatum
food	cibus, cibi (m.)
foolish	stultus, stulta, stultum
forest	silva, silvae (f.)
fortress	castellum, castelli (n.)
free (adj)	liber, libera, liberum
friend (female)	amica, amicae (f.)
friend (male)	amicus, amici (m.)
from	a, ab (+abl.); e, ex (+abl.)

G

game	ludus, ludi (m.)
garden	hortus, horti (m.)
gate	porta, portae (f.)
gem	gemma, gemmae (f.)
gift	donum, doni (n.)
girl	puella, puellae (f.)
give	do, dare, dedi, datum
god	deus, dei (m.)
gold	aurum, auri (n.)
good	bonus, bona, bonum
grain	frumentum, frumenti (n.)
grass	herba, herbae (f.)
grateful	gratus, grata, gratum
great	magnus, magna, magnum
greedy	avarus, avara, avarum
ground	terra, terrae (f.)

H

handsome	pulcher, pulchra, pulchrum
happy	laetus, laeta, laetum
have (verb)	habeo, habēre, habui, habitum
heaven	caelum, caeli (n.)
helmet	galea, galeae (f.)
help (verb)	iuvo, iuvare, iuvi, iutum
herb	herba, herbae (f.)
high	altus, alta, altum
hill	tumulus, tumuli (m.)
hold (verb)	teneo, tenēre, tenui, tentum
holy	sanctus, sancta, sanctum
horrendous	horrendus, horrenda, horrendum
horse	equus, equi (m.)
hot	calidus, calida, calidum
hour	hora, horae (f.)
house	casa, casae (f.)
hunt (verb)	capto, captare, captavi, captatum
hurry (verb)	festino, festinare, festinavi, festinatum

I

in	in (+abl.)
in front of	ob (+acc.); prae (+abl.)
into	in (+acc.)
island	insula, insulae (f.)
Italy	Italia, Italiae (f.)

K	
kill (verb)	neco, necare, necavi, necatum
kitchen	culina, culinae

L	
land	terra, terrae (f.)
large	magnus, magna, magnum
left, left-handed	sinister, sinistra, sinistrum
lie down (verb)	iaceo, iacere, iacui, ---
line	linea, lineae (f.)
little	parvus, parva, parvum
live (verb)	habito, habitare, habitavi, habitatum
long	longus, longa, longum
look at (verb)	specto, spectare, spectavi, spectatum
lord	dominus, domini (m.)
love (verb)	amo, amare, amavi, amatum

M	
man	vir, viri (m.)
many	multus, multa, multum
marketplace	forum, fori (n.)
master	dominus, domini (m.)
mine	meus, mea, meum
moon	luna, lunae (f.)
move (verb)	moveo, movēre, movi, motum
much	multus, multa, multum
my	meus, mea, meum

N	
near	apud (+acc.); iuxta (+acc.); prope (+acc.)
never	numquam
new	novus, nova, novum
next to	iuxta (+acc.)
not	non
now	nunc

O	
ocean	oceanus, oceani (m.)
often	saepe
old	antiquus, antiqua, antiquum
on	in (+abl.)
on account of	propter (+acc.)
on behalf of	pro (+abl.)
onto	in (+acc.)
order (verb)	iubeo, iubēre, iussi, iussum
out of	e, ex (+abl.)
outside of	extra (+acc.)
over	super (+abl. or +acc.)

P	
page	pagina, paginae (f.)
past	praeter (+acc.)
pearl	margarita, margaritae (f.)
pen	stilus, stili (m.)
pirate	pirata, piratae (m.)
place	locus, loci (m.)
plain (level space)	campus, campi (m.)
plant	herba, herbae (f.)
plow (verb)	aro, arare, aravi, aratum
poet	poeta, poetae (m.)
point out (verb)	demonstro, demonstrare, demonstravi, demonstratum
praise (verb)	laudo, laudare, laudavi, laudatum
pray (verb)	oro, orare, oravi, oratum
prepare (verb)	paro, parare, paravi, paratum
prepared (adj.)	paratus, parata, paratum

Q / R	
queen	regina, reginae (f.)
rejoice (verb)	gaudeo, gaudere, gavisus sum, ---
right, right-handed	dexter, dextra, dextrum
river	fluvius, fluvii (m.)
road	via, viae (f.)
Rome	Roma, Romae (f.)
roof	tectum, tecti (n.)
rose (noun)	rosa, rosae (f.)

S

sad	miser, misera, miserum
sail (verb)	navigo, navigare, navigavi, navigatum
sailor	nauta, nautae (m.)
sand	harena, harenae (f.)
school	ludus, ludi (m.)
scribe	scriba, scribae (m.)
sea monster	cetus, ceti (m.)
see	video, videre, vidi, visum
seize (verb)	occupo, occupare, occupavi, occupatum
servant (female)	serva, servae (f.)
servant (male)	servus, servi (m.)
settler	incola, incolae (m.)
shield	scutum, scuti (n.)
shop	taberna, tabernae (f.)
shopkeeper	tabernarius, tabernarii
shout (verb)	clamo, clamare, clamavi, clamatum
silver	argentum, argenti (n.)
sing (verb)	canto, cantare, cantavi, cantatum
sister	germana, germanae (f.)
sit (verb)	sedeo, sedere, sedi, sessum
sky	caelum, caeli (n.)
slave (female)	serva, servae (f.)
slave (male)	servus, servi (m.)
small	parvus, parva, parvum
son	filius, filii (m.)
spear	hasta, hastae (f.)
stand (verb)	sto, stare, steti, statum
star	astrum, astri (n.); stella, -ae (f.)
stay (verb)	maneo, manere, mansi, mansum
story	fabula, fabulae (f.)
straight	rectus, recta, rectum
strange	mirus, mira, mirum
street	via, viae (f.)
string	linea, lineae (f.)
student (female)	discipula, discipulae (f.)
student (male)	discipulus, discipuli (m.)
stylus	stilus, stili (m.)
suitable	aptus, apta, aptum
swim (verb)	nato, natare, natavi, natatum
sword	gladius, gladii (m.)

T

table	mensa, mensae (f.)
tall	altus, alta, altum
teach (verb)	doceo, docere, docui, doctum
teacher (female)	magistra, magistrae (f.)
teacher (male)	magister, magistri (m.)
tell (verb)	narro, narrare, narravi, narratum
temple	templum, templi (n.)
then	tunc
through	per (+acc.)
tired	fessus, fessa, fessum
to	ad (+acc.)
today	hodie
tomorrow	cras
toward	ad (+acc.)
town	oppidum, oppidi (n.)
true	verus, vera, verum

U / V

ugly	foedus, foeda, foedum
under	sub (+abl); sub (+acc. with motion)
up to	sub (+acc.)
upon	super (+abl. or +acc. with motion)
victory	victoria, victoriae (f.)

W

walk (verb)	ambulo, ambulare, ambulavi, ambulatum
wall	murus, muri (m.)
wander (verb)	erro, errare, erravi, erratum
war	bellum, belli (n.)
warm	calidus, calida, calidum

warn (verb)	moneo, monēre, monui, monitum
water	aqua, aquae (f.)
water-carrier	aquarius, aquarii (m.)
way	via, viae (f.)
whale	cetus, ceti (m.)
while	dum
wide	latus, lata, latum
wild	ferus, fera, ferum
wind	ventus, venti (m.)
window	fenestra, fenestrae
wine	vinum, vini (n.)
with	cum (+abl.)
within	intra (+acc.)

without	sine (+abl.)
wolf	lupus, lupi (m.)
woman	femina, feminae (f.)
wonderful	mirus, mira, mirum
woods	silva, silvae (f.)
word	verbum, verbi (n.)
work (verb)	laboro, laborare, laboravi, laboratum
wretched	miser, misera, miserum
Y	
year	annus, anni (m.)
yesterday	heri
your, yours	tuus, tua, tuum

Made in the USA
Columbia, SC
28 December 2018